WHAT CHRISTIAN LEADERS ARE SAYING ABOUT THE SWORD OF THE SPIRIT THE WORD OF GOD

The Sword of The Spirit, The Word of God: **A Handbook for Praying God's Word, by Joy Lamb, is welcomed unanimously by church leaders.**

"What we've been waiting for" is how one leader described *The Sword of the Spirit, The Word of God: A Handbook for Praying God's Word* by Joy Lamb. *"I am convinced that this is the key we have been missing when we pray for healing, salvation, the church, etc.,"* is how Reona Joly of YWAM described the Scriptural prayers in this book.

"Word-centered praying is an absolute must for effective intercession. So is Spirit-led prayer. When the two are combined, something supernatural of God is released against the work of our enemy. The "thank you" prayers-categorized for easy reference in this handbook - make this an invaluable tool towards transformation of lives, cities, and nations. My prayer is for the Holy Spirit to breathe on God's Word in this book, and to inspire the intercession of His children to bring this about. Isaiah 55:11 says it all!" said Brian Mills of InterPrayer.

Not a book to read, a book to use daily! *The Sword of the Spirit, The Word of God* is a powerful tool to use when you pray individually or in a group. It is divided into sections of Scriptural Prayers: for the unity and healing of the Church; salvation; Baptism of the Holy Spirit; physical healing; inner healing; deliverance; relationships; wisdom and guidance; joy and peace; protection; comfort; the peace of Israel; spiritual renewal for our nation; our communities; the world; and special needs. It also includes special prayers for repentance forgiveness, freedom from guilt, salvation, receiving the Holy Spirit, breaking curses, renouncing occult activities, incest survivors and freeing from hereditary sickness.

When confronted with the task of praying for many people with desperate needs, Joy Lamb asked the Lord what to do. She clearly heard: **"Pray My Word, child. It brings healing in all areas. Trust Me and pray My Word."** For more than 21 years she has been obedient to that word. Joy has seen God transform individual lives and communities around the world. Today she is joined by several thousand prayer groups in the US and Europe praying these Scriptures in unity.

Jane Holloway, Prayer Coordinator of the Alliance, described it as *"A timely book that will help many pray more effectively based on God's Word."*

ISBN 978-0-9837058-3-3

Published by Lamb's Books, Inc., P.O. Box 380035, Jacksonville, FL 32205.
Twentieth US Printing Revised - Edition 2018

The Sword of the Spirit the Word of God
**is available at
Amazon.com in print or Kindle versions**

With the free **Kindle App**, *The Sword of the Spirit the Word of God* is available
for download on your tablet, smart phone, or other mobile device, to carry with
you wherever you go. With Kindle you can also use *The Sword of the Spirit the
Word of God* as a reference on your desktop or laptop computer.

Search Amazon.com for *The Sword of the Spirit the Word of God*

email: lambsbooks2@gmail.com
www.theswordofthespiritbook.com

THE SWORD OF THE SPIRIT
THE WORD OF GOD

A Handbook for Praying God's Word

JOY LAMB

It seems good to me to declare the signs and wonders which the Most High God has done for me.

How great are His signs, and how mighty are His wonders. His Kingdom is an everlasting Kingdom, and His Dominion is from generation to generation.

Daniel 4:2-3

Thank You Lord that You will grant Your bond servants to speak Your Word with all confidence, while You will extend Your hand to heal, and signs and wonders will take place through the name of Your Holy Servant Jesus. In the name of JesusChrist.

Acts 4:29-30

Thank You Lord that Your people who are called by Your Name, shall humble themselves, and pray, and seek Your face, and turn from their wicked ways, then You will hear from Heaven, and will forgive their sin, and will heal their land.

2 Chronicles 7:14

In the name of Jesus Christ!

www.theswordofthespiritbook.com

LAMB'S BOOKS, INC.

For Bronson,

My precious husband who has taught me all about God's unconditional love. This book would never have been possible without his love, help, and understanding. On June 23, 2011, Bronson went to be with the Lord Jesus in His Holy Kingdom. May my dear beloved be constantly blessed in Heaven!

Then the Lord said *'Behold I am going to make a covenant. Before all you people I will perform miracles which have not been produced in all the earth nor among any of the nations: and all the people among whom you live will see the working of the Lord, for it is a fearful thing that I am going to perform with you.'*

Exodus 34:10

CONTENTS

ACKNOWLEDGMENTS

I give thanks to the Lord Jesus Christ who lifted me out of the darkness and into the light to participate in the wonder of intercession.

My thanks to Jerry Shriner, Alma Coit, Connie Green, Frances Hanusek, Ann Bauwens, Barbara Newman, Mercy Jones, Pat Zink, Jill Wilson, Betty Heindel, Norma Dearing, Joy Abney, Dave Busse, Francis MacNutt, Thyrza Zabriskie, Michele Perry, Grace Sarber, Louise Allen, Patricia Phillips, Rosemary Phillips, Monet Kent, Anne Early, Harriett Lovejoy, Pat Smith, Ellen Geuther, Mary Ann Lewis-my assistant, and all CHM Intercessors who prayed that this intercessory handbook would become a reality, and be used to the glory of God.

INTRODUCTION

I have discovered that praying for the needs of God's people is one of life's most fulfilling and rewarding experiences. When we come to the Lord in prayer we are given a unique opportunity to see His power and love at work in our lives, and in the lives and situations for which we are praying.

The Sword of The Spirit - The Word of God has been an exciting adventure. After I received a great deal of inner healing through the prayers of Francis and Judith MacNutt, I became a volunteer for Christian Healing Ministries. Within several weeks I became aware of a growing basket of letters in the lunch room. I was told that they were prayer requests the MacNutts had received from around the world. Their busy schedules made it impossible for them to pray for all these requests individually. They were thrilled when I asked if I could take responsibility for them. I took these letters to the chapel and asked the Lord what I should do. He spoke clearly to me saying, "Pray My Word, child. It brings healing in all areas. Trust Me and pray My Word."

I began to categorize the many requests according to the needs of the people. As I read over the names in each category, Scripture verses seemed to jump off the pages of my Bible. It was so exciting watching the Holy Spirit at work in this powerful way. This became such a powerful method to pray for hundreds of people in a very short time. Leave it to God to make it simple.

Three friends and I began praying the Scriptures for each category of prayer needs on a regular basis. We decided to respond to each individual letting them know we were praying for them. We asked that they would let us know of any answered prayers. The praise reports began almost immediately. People were seeing the power of praying God's Word in their lives. They began to request copies of the "categorized" Scriptural prayers in order to pray for others. Within months, our prayer group of three quickly grew to more than five-hundred intercessors. This was the birth of *The Sword of The Spirit The Word of God:* A Handbook for Praying God's Word.

In 1989, I felt the Holy Spirit nudging me to gather a group dedicated to praying God's Word for the healing of the land. The vision for this book is to cover America and the world with God's Holy Word as people pray in a symphony of unity for the healing of the world.

What has happened over the past several years has been amazing. We have never advertised. We do not have a publisher, distributor or promoter. However, the books go out daily by the case loads to individuals, churches of all denominations, prisons, prayer groups and counseling centers throughout the world. At present there are thousands of prayer groups praying God's Holy Word in one accord. I stand in awe as I watch this happen. I am reminded that from the very beginning this was begun in obedience to God's call.

As intercessors, we are commissioned by God to be anxious for nothing but in everything, by prayer and petition and with thanksgiving make our requests known to Him. We are in a battle against the spiritual forces of evil in the heavenly realm that would try to destroy the church, Christian institutions, families, value systems, governments, the environment, our health and our world. My prayer is that intercessory groups would continue to emerge throughout the world in every facet of our lives and that through prayer, God would continue to bring healing and love to our world, binding up and tearing down the strongholds of satan. May we speak God's word with confidence.

Thank You Lord that You will grant that Your bond servants will speak Your Word with all confidence, while You extend Your hand to heal, and signs and wonders will take place through the name of Your holy servant Jesus.

Acts 4:29-30

Joy Lamb

Dear Intercessors,

It has been my great joy these last twenty four years to make *The Sword of the Spirit, The Word of God* available to you as a tool for prayer. The Lord has recently given me something to use in my personal prayer time which I believe will enhance your intercession as well.

For several years I have been dealing with a challenge to my vision. Now I understand that this challenge has been gift from God and I thank Him for it. Because it had become increasingly difficult for me to read the prayers from the book, I made voice recordings of several portions of *The Sword of the Spirit* so I can listen to the prayers instead of reading them. As I listen, I pray in the Spirit and/or praise God.

I am finding that this is a phenomenal way to pray, combining God's word in spoken prayer with Spirit prayer. I am also finding that having the prayers easily accessible on my smartphone enables me to use ear buds so I can listen and pray this way anytime, anywhere.

I am making these audio prayers available to you on Lamb's Books' website, free of charge. I am asking that, if you feel led to do so, you would recommend these audio prayers to other intercessors. Since the beginning, my vision for *Sword of the Spirit* has always been to cover this land with the Word of God for the healing of the nation, to mobilize Intercessors to pray the Word in unity. I do encourage you as you listen and pray these prayers to pray the Deliverance-Protection prayer for yourself daily. (This prayer is found on pages 25-26)

In recent months the Lord has been speaking to me about the power of forgiveness and our great need to live a lifestyle of forgiveness. In this new edition of *Sword of the Spirit* I have added a National Forgiveness Prayer on page 20. You will also find an audio version of the National Forgiveness Prayer on **LAMB'S BOOKS' WEBSITE: www.theswordofthespiritbook.com**. I encourage you to also pray through the Forgiveness Prayers (pp. 18-20) from time to time because it is forgiveness that empowers, heals and sets free.

Joy Lamb

A testimony on deliverance from a Pastor in Kentucky

The book, *The Sword of the Spirit - The Word of God* by Joy Lamb is far more than a must read for all Christians. It is a must have weapon of spiritual warfare that needs to be in the possession of each and every serious Christian. Tragically the church has discarded and lost many important values through the years. And when we as a church lose them it not only affects us as the Body of Christ but also robs the lives of people in our paths and future generations who have no knowledge of them. Deliverance is one of those things that I believe has been nearly lost along the way. Deliverance is very scriptural. As stated in Matthew 6:13; The Lord's Prayer says "but deliver us from evil".

Before becoming a pastor I served as an altar worker in a very large church. One evening at an altar call I was praying for several people. When I left the church that night I realized something was really very wrong with me spiritually. On the way home I gradually developed a nearly uncontrolled rage that scared everyone in the car. I prayed hard while driving and was unsuccessful to deliver myself from the evil that was now in me. My wife and I planned to deal with the issue just as soon as we got home. The plan was for me to go up into our prayer room and to pray to cast out the evil spirit.

I desperately raced up the stairs to our prayer room. By now I knew the intent of the evil spirit upon me. It was trying hard to force me to murder my family. I sat down on the canopy bed in the prayer room, struggling very much to keep myself under control. I reached for my Sword of the Spirit book that was lying on that bed. Before I could grasp it, suddenly a nearly overwhelming urge came over me to jump up and go and murder my family. With all my might I resisted and cried out, "Jesus help me!" Not by my might but by His I grabbed one of the bedposts and stopped. I was then able to get on my knees and begin reading the "Deliverance Prayer" on page 25 of The Sword of the Spirit. I shakily read through the first four paragraphs of that prayer and I felt the release of the evil that was trying its best to destroy me. I finished that prayer and rejoiced because I had the victory over the devil. By the power of God's promises in that prayer I experienced deliverance from the evil spirit in me and the devil was stopped from harming me and my family in ways that would have been irreversible. I owe a huge debt of gratitude to Joy Lamb for bringing that prayer to me and my family.

Pastor Milton Jelley

TESTIMONIES OF INTERCESSORS USING THE SWORD OF THE SPIRIT, THE WORD OF GOD:

I would like to share with you a small sample of intercessor praise reports:

- Back in 2009 God brought me out of a bad place and I started digging into His word more and using scripture for my declarations in warfare over my children and myself and my household. I would write down scripture and His promises and personalize them for myself. I would have pages I would read and declare and pray out loud personalized for me and my children and my family and others.

  One day I was at Goodwill in 2010 looking through their books, and saw one called *The Sword of the Spirit*. Of course the title alone caught my eye. I pulled it out, opened it up, and I was so in awe. I thought to myself, "This is exactly the book I would write if I were going to write a prayer book!" What I loved about your book is that it's all scripture, it's categorized, and you can use it for groups or individuals. I immediately knew I had to share this book with others, so I bought a case and kept them in my car to hand out to people at church, friends and anyone the Lord leads me to...My book is so worn, color tabs everywhere, highlights and all.

  I have since gotten involved in a healing, equipping and deliverance ministry called RLI (Restoring Lives International). I went through my first week long conference with them in Jan 2012 and afterwards I joined the team. They do complete teaching, healing and deliverance based on God's word, teach His truth about open doors to sin and sickness, generational, body, soul, spirit connection and complete Salvation SOZO. Then set people free with deliverance as well as walking it out. Our prayer team prays over our leaders and teachers when they are speaking as well as conference attendees. *The Sword of the Spirit* is my all-time go-to prayer book. I can pray scripture for our teachers under the wisdom section as well as protection, I pray for attendees under the inner healing and deliverance sections, sometimes I pray the generational prayers when we are doing generational healing.

At our last conference in September (2017) we used *The Sword of the Spirit* in the sanctuary during deliverance and our lead Pastor said she could just feel the shift in the room, it was so powerful. Praise be to Jesus!!

Our prayer team uses other books too, but *Sword of the Spirit* is my favorite, because to me it's the most like a bow and arrow. We have the bow, and depending on the need, we choose which arrow (scripture) is best suited to the situation or circumstance. With the way the scriptures are grouped (and I have mine tabbed and highlighted) I can shoot multiple arrows in a short time to cover a variety of situations. I LOVE it. So God anointed! I feel like a real warrior on the spiritual battle ground.

- 'I want to thank you so much for your book. Since I have been praying your prayers of inner healing and deliverance several people I know have decided to come out of the gay lifestyle. One client has made a commitment to the Lord and is participating in an ex-gay ministry and giving a marvellous testimony of what Jesus can do in a person's life! His life alone would have been worth your book. Thank you!'

- 'I am in prison, and I use your book, *The Sword of The Spirit*. There is so much evil in the prisons, but when I pray the deliverance prayers in the book, things get so much calmer and I don't experience the fear I once did. I pray that prayer a lot lately.'

- 'The first morning that I picked up your book and prayed the prayers of deliverance the Lord's anointing was there. Amazing! I know His blessing is on your ministry there, and I wish to encourage you in all that you are doing.'

- 'We used *The Sword of The Spirit* in our chapel service (we are Methodists). We have never felt the power of God so strongly. What a blessing this has been for us. Thank you.'

- 'Our prayer life has been energized by your book. Due to your splendid scripture selections and your topics going to the heart of prayer, it is a fine tool to have for years to come. Intercession is the most rewarding service of all, that has been my experience, and it is certainly more so since using your book.'

- 'I am a member of Catholics in Action. We have been praying for families, Government leaders, Church leaders and all needs of each other. I have passed *The Sword of The Spirit* around and need more. What miracles are happening!'

- 'I want to express my thanks to you for offering your book of scriptural references, *The Sword of The Spirit*, to use with prayer groups. I have had so many answers to praying scripture that my faith is high. Recently my husband became a believer using these prayers. We prayed then for our son who was having trouble in school. His entire situation was reversed within a few days.'

- 'Since I have become an intercessor, it seems everything is falling into place. I love the book, *The Sword of The Spirit*. I read the whole book every day. When I ordered the book, one of my grandsons was running with the wrong crowd, he had become a member of a group who follows a very famous rock group. He got into smoking pot and we think selling it. He started all this at 16 years old. He got so bad his parents had to put him out of the house. After six months, he went back home and asked for forgiveness. Now he is doing real well. His parents were on the brink of divorce. All of our intercessors have been praying. It looks like everything is finally coming together. Peace in the home. I am so thankful for all the prayers, and for your book.'

- 'Your book is wonderful. I really appreciate your giving us a copy. My stepson had just been killed in a car accident, and there was such a heaviness around me and I couldn't pray. I took your book and prayed the long deliverance prayer and everything immediately broke from over me. Now, praying is once again a joy. We are also using it in our intercession group. It has helped us to become more organized so that we accomplish much more.'

- 'You know at the meeting last week, we had quite a diverse group of denominations in our Women Aglow group, and all were touched by your book. There were Catholics, lots of Lutherans, Episcopalians, Methodists, Baptists and Charismatics. Your book has overwhelmed all of us.'

- 'I am a victim of severe childhood sexual abuse, and as result have suffered most of my life with Multiple Personality Disorders with very little results from counseling. I wrote you and asked for prayer, you sent me a copy of *The Sword of The Spirit*. After a few weeks of praying the Deliverance scriptures and prayer, my personalities are beginning to merge, and I feel better than I have in years. Your book has meant life to me.'

- 'Thanking God as we ask in prayer really touched my heart. This form of prayer is truly scriptural. I'm in my fourth year of the Catholic Biblical School. It's tremendous and very thorough and faith centered. Many marriages have been saved and relationships healed. We see hearts softened towards Jesus and the faith they were brought up in. I have distributed these books to priests who are very touched. They love it when we say we are interceding for them and their staffs. These prayers broaden your love for the whole world and create greater concern for prayer for media, schools and government.'

- 'I have been so blessed by the *The Sword of The Spirit*. I use it daily. I have no prayer group here so I use it individually daily to do spiritual warfare. I am especially blessed by the forgiveness prayers and am seeing new freedom in myself as I am forgiving over and over those I need to forgive.'

- 'I am so grateful to be an intercessor. It is a wonderful blessing to pray the Scriptures every day. Thank you so much for encouraging me to do so. I have been faithfully praying the Deliverance Prayer and Scriptures for those on my daily list. I have also noticed satan's multiple attacks when I miss a day, so God has used that 'unpaid servant' to make me disciplined!'

- 'During the many years that I have been 'a pray-er' I have learned how powerful it is to pray God's Word back to Him. I also have experienced the power of praise as a personal attitude (and sometimes discipline!) But Joy, I had never phrased Scripture as praise and promise the way you have done in *The Sword of The Spirit*. I feel the anointing every time I pray! Thank you for sharing this gift with me and all of us. CHM represents to me one of the most balanced and powerful ministries. I feel privileged to pray and be part of the healing and reaching out to the many people who are searching for Jesus these days.'

- 'I am writing you to thank you for the privilege of being one of your new intercessors. The first time I made intercession for the request sent to me as part of my morning devotion, I felt lightened and blessed, and I continue to feel good about it.'

- 'My wife and I minister regularly at prisons. Recently we have been ministering in the realms of deliverance. Your book fits like a piece of a puzzle in the midst of all that we are doing. Your book, *The Sword of The Spirit*, has definitely been inspired by the Spirit of God.'

- 'I am soaring each morning as I pray with the *The Sword of The Spirit*.'

- 'Your book *The Sword of The Spirit* has been a great inspiration to me – and great help. Recently, while sharing the deliverance prayer with a friend, he asked how we could get more copies. I am an ex-gay involved in an ex-gay ministry and we feel this book could be of great benefit to all our leaders and members.'

- 'I am in prison for life. I am holding the book *The Sword of The Spirit* in my hand right now. I cannot tell you what this book has meant to me. It seems God has already started doing a mighty work in my life. I would like to send a letter to the young generation and let them know that they can stop and turn their life around before it is too late or they end up in a situation like I am in. However, it seems I'm okay now. I have this feeling of hope. Thank you again for this book.'

- 'Years ago when looking for a scripture text that would describe the task of an intercessor, I opened 'by accident' to Isaiah 62:6-7 and I've often used the text in writing or in preaching and then recently a copy of the excellent book *The Sword of The Spirit* fell into my hands. CLICK – all the parts all fit together. Your book and 'my' text seem made for each other. The book is made up of God's promises. The Isaiah text calls on us to remind God of his promises. We have been given a voice that He must heed namely His Word. I look forward to mounting the walls of Jerusalem to do my round of duty!'

- 'For the past 30 days I have been reading *The Sword of The Spirit*. I cannot begin to tell you the wonders the book has done for me. I became a Jewish believer in 'Yeshua' (Jesus) over one year ago. I have been in prison over 14 years and only after being born again, have I finally found peace.'

- 'Thank you for this wonderful book that has helped me grow in my prayer life. I found the prayers to be very powerful and healing. When a member of my family was going through a very difficult illness, I prayed the Prayer of Deliverance and miraculous things happened. Just praying the prayer has also helped me to heal from some long standing deep seated painful memories. I appreciate the dedication and love that went into this God inspired book of prayers.'

- 'After ordering one copy of *Sword of the Spirit* at a time to give people, I ordered a case. Several new people were voicing interest in prayer ministry so I gave them copies and briefly walked them through the book. Our little Thursday night prayer group that prays over our church prayer chain often reads from *The Sword of the Spirit* during those two hours. This book is making a tremendous impact on our church.'

****

The 'Answered Prayers' (p. 172) are testimonies of people who have written or called in for prayer. Our intercessors prayed Scripture for them using *The Sword of The Spirit*. We have hundreds of these testimonies, a true blessing from our Lord, but I feel that this is only the beginning of what He is about to do as we turn to Him in His Word.

Jesus was led by the Spirit into the desert to be tempted by the devil. Although Jesus was the Son of God, He defeated Satan by using a weapon that everyone has at his disposal: the sword of the Spirit which is the word of God (Ephesians 6:17). He met all three temptations with Scriptural truth. (Deut 8:3).*

God's Word has been written and preserved through the ages for such
a time as this. It is available to each
of us to defeat Satan in every area of our lives.

Take up your sword!

* NIV Study Bible- Study Notes Matthew 4:1-11 Zondervan

THE WORD

In the beginning was the Word, and the Word was with God, and the Word was God. He was in the beginning with God.

John 1:1-2

For the Lord will execute His Word upon the earth thoroughly and quickly.

Romans 9:28

The sum of Thy Word is truth and every one of Thy righteous ordinances is everlasting.

Psalms 119:60

God is His Word and praying God's Word is speaking the very being of God into the situation. Meditating upon His Word causes truth, Spirit and power to become integrated with our own beings and with the being for whom we are interceding. Speaking His truth, His Love, His power brings knowledge, cleansing, healing, and wholeness. It brings peace and unexplainable joy – it brings freedom!

Whatever the need, great or small, God's Word has the answer. Take the sword of the Spirit, which is the Word of God (Eph 6:17). This sword, the Word of God, is to be used as a powerful weapon against satan and all the powers of darkness. It is to be used to open all people's eyes so that they may turn from darkness to light and from the dominion of satan to God, in order that they might receive forgiveness of sins and an inheritance among those who have been sanctified by faith in Jesus Christ (see Acts26:18).

It is to be used to tear down strongholds, to build up, to heal, to set captives free, and to seek and save those who are lost.

God has this to say about His Word:

But to this one I will look. To him who is humble and contrite of spirit, and who trembles at My Word.

Isaiah 66:2

Then the Lord said to me, you have seen well, for I am watching over My Word to perform it.

Jeremiah 1:12

Blessed are those who hear the Word of God and observe it.

Luke 11:12

My son, give attention to My Words; incline your ear to My Sayings. Do not let them depart from your sight; keep them in the midst of your heart, for they are life to those that find them, and health to all their whole body.

Proverbs 4:20-22

Jesus might sanctify Her (the Church), having cleansed Her, by the washing of water with the Word.

Ephesians 5:26

It is easier for heaven and earth to pass away than for one stroke of a letter of the Law to fail.

Luke 16:17

For the Word of God is living and active and sharper than any two edged sword, and piercing as far as the division of soul and spirit, of both joints and marrow, and able to judge the thoughts and intentions of the heart. And there is no creature hidden from His sight, but all things are open and laid bare to the eyes of Him with whom we have to do.

Hebrews 4:12-13

Thank You Lord that all Scripture is inspired by God and profitable for teaching, for reproof, for correction, for training in righteousness; that the men of God may be adequately equipped for every good work. In the name of Jesus Christ.

2 Timothy 3:16-17

The Lord worked with them, and confirmed the Word by the signs that followed.

Mark 16:20

Is not My Word like a fire says the Lord, and like a hammer that shatters a rock.

Jeremiah 23:29

He who gives attention to the Word shall find good, and blessed is he who trusts in the Lord.

Proverbs 16:20

May Your loving kindness also come to me, Oh Lord, Your salvation according to Your Word. I shall have an answer for him, for I trust in Your Word.

Psalm 119:41-42

For as the rain and snow come down from heaven, and do not return there without watering the earth, and making it bear, and sprout, and furnishing seed to the sower, and bread to the eater: so shall My Word be, which goes forth from My mouth, it shall not return to Me empty, without accomplishing what I desire, and without succeeding in the matter for which I sent it.

Isaiah 55:10-11

For this reason we also constantly thank God, that when you received from us the Word of God's message, you accepted it not as the word of men, but for what it really is, the Word of God, which also performs its work in you who believe.

I Thessalonians 2:13

We have heard the Word in an honest and good heart, and hold it fast, and bear fruit with perseverance.

Luke 8:15

Whoever keeps His Word, in Him the love of God has truly been perfected. By this we know that we are in Him.

I John 2:5

And He is clothed with a robe dipped in blood; and His name is called The Word of God. (*Description of Jesus Christ*).

Revelation 19:13

If you abide in Me, and My Words abide in you, ask whatever you wish, and it shall be done for you. By this is My Father glorified, that you bear much fruit, and so prove to be My disciples.

John15:7-8

It is clear why God establishes such power in Scriptural prayer, using His Word, the Sword of the Spirit, as the most powerful weapon to destroy the enemy.

SUGGESTED GUIDELINES
FOR GROUP INTERCESSION

Appoint a regular time, once a week or once a month, which is agreeable to all involved. Remember when two or three are gathered together in His name, Jesus is in their midst: consequently, two can be 'the group'.

Commit to coming together at this time. Let this commitment always be a first priority. Do not be tempted to make any other appointments or commitments during this time.

Appoint a leader, but with the understanding that all involved will share leadership. Allow a different person to lead the group from time to time, but keep the format the same. Commit to praying God's Word as a group, as well as individually.

Set a time limit and stick to it. This time should be used for prayer only. Save visiting and talking until after the group session, otherwise your intercession time can quickly become a gossip session.

- **Come together in total silence.**

- **Invite the Holy Spirit** to guide you in your prayer time.

- **Ask the Lord's forgiveness** for all known and unknown sins of the group. Silently confess any unforgiveness that you may be harboring, 'lest your prayers be hindered.' (See Forgiveness Prayer pages 18-19)

- This is also an excellent time to **pray the Deliverance Prayer** (pp. 25-27) or you can pray it at the end.

As you become a prayer warrior, you may experience some interference from satan and his allies. Satan is not pleased when God's army begins to pray against him and will no doubt plan a counter attack.

Consequently, you may want to get into the daily habit of binding the power of satan in your life, your family's lives, and your work places. I try to remember the saying 'if the devil can't make you bad, he will make you too busy.' The deliverance prayer is especially beneficial when prayed at the beginning of your intercessory group meeting for the members of the group and their families.

- **Pray the Intercessors Cree**d (p. 13).

- **Then pray a few Scriptures for Intercessors** (p. 14).

- **Write the individual requests (first names only) on the Prayer Request Form**. This form may be copied and enlarged for easier use. There is a sample copy (p. 11) and a copy for personal use (p. 12).

  Consistently state the importance of confidentiality in all petitions. Always strive to be a trustworthy intercessor. Use first names only when praying for others.

- **Identify the needs** as salvation, physical healing, inner healing, special needs, deliverance, relationships, protection and comfort, wisdom and guidance, faith and strength, joy and peace.

- After all the requests have been put on the form, **lift the names to the Lord, praying several Scriptural Prayers** where they apply.

- **Close with the Deliverance Prayer** (p. 25) if you did not pray it earlier.

- After intercession or prayer with laying on of hands, please pray the **Cutting Free Prayer** (p. 31). Very Important!

This prayer sets your own spirit free from any burden bearing after intercession that could cause oppression, depression or even illness. If the intercession becomes intense, the need for this will be important. The Lord does not want you to carry the burdens of another. He wants you to release the person to Him, in order for the Lord to do His work in the person for whom you are praying. Releasing the person to the Lord is one key to healing, desperately hanging on to a person often prevents God's intervention.

Commit to praying for these petitions on the Prayer Request Form (p. 12) individually three to four times a week for three weeks to a month, then let the names go. Depending on how often you meet, you will be adding names throughout the month. Placing a date by the names will facilitate your knowing when to take names off the list. The little yellow stickies are very useful for listing names on the Scripture pages.

Fasting can be one of the most powerful tools of intercession. In difficult situations, fasting can make a significant breakthrough. This takes commitment and discipline, but the results are phenomenal. A one-day fast seems to be sufficient. Omit breakfast and lunch. This is very little to sacrifice, but experience has shown that God honors the commitment.

Please pray the Scriptures and fast for the unity of the Church (p. 58), Israel (p. 65), your community (p. 81), the nation and worldwide issues (p. 68). There are several thousand prayer groups fasting and praying for the nation and the Church using Scriptures from *The Sword of The Spirit, The Word of God*. Please join us.

Remember, these suggestions are not absolutes, for there is no set way of praying; but when you are praying for people and situations at a distance, this type of intercession seems to work best.

We have found that praying the Deliverance Prayer and the Scriptures over people in the different categories is very powerful and is in God's will, for Scripture tells us that Jesus was sent to destroy the works of the devil, and God will not let His Word return void and He is quick to perform it (Isaiah 55:10-11).

We stand on the powerful promises of God's Word. We have also found that in praying this way, one can pray for many people in a short period of time. Remember, simply lift up the names to the Lord, pray the Scriptures, followed by the Deliverance Prayers, then let it go. Trust and let the Lord do His work through His Word. 'The Lord will work with us and confirm the Word by the signs that follow' (Mark 16:20).

INDIVIDUAL INTERCESSION

Commit to praying at least three times a week. Choose the same time and place on the appointed days. If you find it hard to find the time, ask the Lord to waken you earlier on those 'committed' days. He will do it.

Read and meditate on the Scriptures for a few minutes, allowing yourself to come into the presence of the Lord. You may wish to keep a journal, jotting down the Lord's responses. What a joy this can be.

- **Invite the Holy Spirit** to guide your prayer time.

- **Pray the Intercessors Creed** (p. 13).

- **Pray the Scriptures for Intercessors** (p. 14).

- Take the **Prayer Request Form** (p. 12). This form may be copied and enlarged for easier use.

- **Write the names** of the people you want to pray for under the appropriate categories on the Prayer Request Form.

- Lift up the names of the people on your Prayer Request Form by praying several, or all, of the relevant **Scriptural Prayers** over them.

- **Pray the Deliverance Prayer** (p. 25) over all for whom you have prayed the Scriptural Prayers. (Pray it just once over all the names). Speaking these names and prayers out loud is very powerful.

- Please remember to **pray for the unity of the Church (p. 58), Israel (p. 65), your community (p. 81), the nation and worldwide issues (p. 76).**

- After intercession or 'hands on' intercession, you may find it helpful to **pray the Cutting Free Prayer** (p. 31).

Watch each day how the Lord will bless you with His love and presence. You will be amazed how lives will be changed as a result of obedience to intercession (see 2 Chronicles 7:14).

Do not limit yourselves to pray only for the requests that you receive. If we all unite as intercessors, praying God's Word in one accord, there is no limit to the victory of the light overcoming the darkness. Pray Deliverance Prayers and Scriptures against the evil that has the potential for causing destruction and division to our nation, our families, our government, our churches, our schools, our youth, our Christian beliefs. On pages 76-80 are suggested topics.

I have chosen these groups and factions simply from the standpoint that if what they represent, or condone, is not in concordance with God's Word, then they are out of the will of God, and therefore, 'in the will of satan to do his work' (2 Tim 2:26).

The lists on pages 76-80 are only partial lists of the many people and organizations that the Lord wants to draw unto Himself. Be on the alert as you go throughout your daily activities. The Lord will consistently nudge you to pray for certain people, groups, institutions, and organizations.

Please remember as you pray for these groups that God created every one of these people in love. Every person comes from God, they are here on earth to serve God, and one day they will return to God. We as intercessors are never to judge or condemn another human being. That is God's task, and His alone. We are only to pray for them, to lift them to the Lord in love. If anyone is in sin, we are to love the sinner but hate the sin.

Jesus Christ appeared in order to take away sins; and in Jesus there is no sin.

1 John 3:5

Unanswered Prayer

A word about unanswered prayer. This topic has been the 'unanswered topic' forever. No one seems to have the answer; however, I have experienced this: if a person does not choose to get well, praying for healing doesn't seem to make a breakthrough. Our heavenly Father has given all of us free will - the right to choose - and this is also true of healing. The person in question could have experienced rejection or trauma as far back as the womb, or may be carrying deep guilt from some woundedness or unconfessed sin. It is my belief that both can result in the person being filled with guilt and/or shame, thus the person never feels worthy of healing. Subconsciously, dying may be their choice rather than healing. In situations with these characteristics, it takes in-depth inner healing to bring about a deep awakening, and an unquestionable knowledge of God's forgiveness and His unconditional love to give the person the desire to live, and thus receive healing. When this happens, the person finally realizes that yes, they were chosen by God, that they are here on earth to serve God, and one day they will go back to God. Knowing this gives life true meaning.

HOW TO USE THIS BOOK

The Sword of the Spirit is not a book to read, but a book to use daily for prayer purposes either in a group or individually. It is divided into sections of Scriptural Prayers for the unity and healing of the Church, salvation, baptism of the Holy Spirit, physical healing, inner healing deliverance, relationships, wisdom and guidance, joy and peace, protection and comfort, the peace of Israel, spiritual renewal for our nation, our communities, the world, and special needs. In this edition we have added text and scriptures for Teenagers and Youth of the Nation, and Generational Healing.

Please look at page 11 and see the SAMPLE COPY of your prayer request form. Note how names are listed. On page 12 you will find a prayer request form that you tear out and print several copies for you and prayer partners. When you are choosing people and categories for which to pray, simply list first names only under appropriate categories, then lift the names to the Lord and turn to the page number of the particular category for which you are praying and pray three or four scriptures from each category. Then close all petitions with the Deliverance Prayer page 25, and the Cutting Free Prayer on page 31. I also find it very comforting to pray Putting on the Full Armor of God (p. 16).

When one prays this way, simply "roll calling" God's children, you can pray for a multitude of people in a very short time. You will be amazed at the POWER in praying God's Word! May God richly bless you as you watch the miracles unfold.

As I stated earlier, I encourage fasting Tuesdays or Wednesdays, only breakfast and lunch and pray for the issues on pages 76-80. I am in a prayer group of three people that is amazing. One person lifts the names silently, while the other one prays the scriptures silently and the third one, who is 1500 miles away, prays the Deliverance Prayer and the Cutting Free Prayer. No one knows who is praying what but we all finish at the exact time! Truly amazing Holy Spirit Unity.

PRAYER REQUEST FORM

Using *The Sword of The Spirit, The Word of God*, write the first names of the people who need prayer. A prayer lists looks like this:

Salvation p. 88 Baptism of The Holy Spirit p. 94	Generational Healing p. 162	Inner/Emotional Healing p. 99	Physical Healing p. 105	Deliverance p. 113	Relationships p. 123
Muslims Jews Buddhists Hindus	Brown family Joanne Stephenson family Bryan	Ed Marie Kristie	Joanne Jeff George	Mike Nathan Kelley	Bob-Sue Debra-Michael Steve-Rhonda
Wisdom and Guidance p. 129	Faith and Strength p. 140	Joy and Peace p. 143	Protection and Comfort pp. 147/150	Blessings of the Lord p. 168	Church p. 58 Israel p. 65 All Nations p. 68 Your City p. 81
Mary Wade Rick	Anne Ted Randal	Candy Jackson Will	Kevin David	Michelle Henry Donna	

Praise for answered prayer (date of answer)	Special needs (Jobs, legal matters, God's choice for a mate, Buying/selling homes, financial blessings) p. 152
	Sally - mate of God's choice Linda - to sell house Joe - financial blessing

SAMPLE COPY

Please close all intercession with the Deliverance Prayer (p. 25). - Cutting Free Prayer (p. 31) - Full Armor of God (p. 16)
Please join intercessors across the nation who are fasting Tues. or Weds (breakfast & lunch) as we pray for the Church and our Nations.
Lamb's Books, Inc. gives permission to photocopy & enlarge this page.

PRAYER REQUEST FORM

Using *The Sword of The Spirit*, *The Word of God*, write the first names of the people for whom you want prayer under the appropriate categories

Salvation p. 88 Baptism of The Holy Spirit p. 94 Muslims, Jews, Hindus, Buddhists	Generational Healing p. 162	Inner/Emotional Healing p. 99	Physical Healing p. 105	Deliverance p. 113 Terrorists Protesters	Relationships p. 123
Wisdom and Guidance p. 129	Faith and Strength p. 140	Joy and Peace p. 143	Protection and Comfort pp. 147/150	Blessings of the Lord p. 168	Church p. 58 Israel p. 65 All Nations p. 68 Your City p. 81
Praise for answered prayer (date of answer)			Special needs (Jobs, legal matters, God's choice for a mate, Buying/selling homes, financial blessings) p. 152		

Please close all intercession with the Deliverance Prayer (p. 25). - Cutting Free Prayer (p. 31) - Full Armor of God (p. 16)

Please join intercessors across the nation who are fasting Tues. or Weds (breakfast & lunch) as we pray for the Church and our Nations.

Lamb's Books, Inc. gives permission to photocopy & enlarge this page.

SPECIAL PRAYERS
INTERCESSOR'S CREED

Thank You Lord that I did not choose You, but You chose me, and appointed me that I should go and bear fruit, and that my fruit should remain, that whatever I ask of the Father in Your name, He may give to me. In the name of Jesus Christ.

John 15:16

Lord I believe that all things I ask in prayer believing, I shall receive. In the name of Jesus Christ.

Matthew 21:22

Thank You Lord that I believe in You and the works that You did I will do, and even greater works than what You, Jesus, did, I will do, because You are with the Father, and whatever I ask in Jesus' name, that will He do, that the Father might be glorified in the Son. In the name of Jesus Christ.

John 14:12-14

Thank You Lord that we believe that You are the God that gives life to the dead, and calls into being that which does not exist. In the name of Jesus Christ.

Romans 4:17

Thank You Lord that we believe that our tongues will bring healing and our tongues will be a tree of Life. In the name of Jesus Christ.

Proverbs 15:4

Thank You Lord that we as intercessors will build up the wall and stand before You in the gap on behalf of America, so You would not have to destroy our Nation. In the name of Jesus Christ.

Ezekiel 22:30

I will do this also!

INTERCESSORS' SCRIPTURES

The following Scriptures are prayed by the intercessors for their fellow intercessors.

Thank You Lord that You will sanctify us in the truth. **Thy Word is truth**. In the name of Jesus Christ.

John 17:17

Thank You Lord that You will work with us and confirm **The Word** by the signs that follow. In the name of Jesus Christ.

Mark 16:20

Thank You Lord that the power of the Lord will be present unto us for Jesus to perform healing. In the name of Jesus Christ.

Luke 5:17

Thank You Lord that You will fulfill all of our petitions. In the name of Jesus Christ.

Psalm 20:5

Thank You Lord that You have heard us and You have attended to the voice of our prayers. Blessed be God who has not turned away our prayers or His mercy from us. In the name of Jesus Christ.

Psalm 66:19-20

Thank You Lord that we are strong, and the Word of God abides in us, and we have overcome the evil one. In the name of Jesus Christ.

1 John 2:14

Thank You Lord that You will strengthen us with power through Your Spirit in our inner man. In the name of Jesus Christ.

Ephesians 3:16

Thank You Lord that we will devote ourselves to prayer, and ministry of the Word. In the name of Jesus Christ.

Acts 6:4

Thank You Lord that we will cast out demons by the finger of God, then the Kingdom of God will come upon us. In the name of Jesus Christ.

Luke 11:20

Thank You Lord that the prayer offered in faith will restore the one who is sick, and the Lord will raise him up, and if he has committed sins, they will be forgiven him. Therefore, we will confess our sins to one another, and pray for one another, so that they may be healed. The effective prayer of a righteous man can accomplish much. In the name of Jesus Christ.

James 5:15-16

Thank You Lord that we will apply our hearts to discipline and our ears to words of knowledge in our prayer time. In the name of Jesus Christ.

Proverbs 23:12

Thank You Lord that You will anoint all intercessors with the Holy Spirit and power as You did Jesus of Nazareth, so that we will go about doing good, and healing all who are oppressed by the devil; for God is with us. In the name of Jesus Christ.

Acts 10:38

Thank You Lord that You will grant that Your bond servants will speak Your Word with all confidence, while You will extend Your hand to heal, and signs and wonders take place through the name of Your Holy Servant Jesus. And when we pray, the place where we gather together will shake and we all will be filled with the Holy Spirit and begin to speak the Word of God with boldness. In the name of Jesus Christ.

Acts 4:29-31

Thank You Lord that Your eyes are open and Your ears are attentive to the prayers in this place. In the name of Jesus Christ.

II Chronicles 6:42

PUTTING ON THE FULL ARMOR OF GOD

- Finally, I will be strong in the Lord, and in the strength of His might:

- I will put on the full armor of God, that I may be able to stand firm against the schemes of the devil.

- For my struggle is not against flesh and blood, but against the rulers, against the powers, against the world forces of this darkness, against the spiritual forces of wickedness in the heavenly places.

- Therefore I will take up the full armor of God, that I may be able to resist in the evil day, and having done everything to stand firm.

- I will stand firm therefore, having girded my loins with truth and having put on the breastplate of righteousness, and having shod my feet with the preparation of the Gospel of Peace. In addition to all, I will take the shield of faith with which I will be able to extinguish all the flaming missiles of the evil one.

- And I will take the helmet of salvation, and the Sword of the Spirit, which is the Word of God, with all prayer and petition. I will pray at all times in the Spirit, and with this in view I will be on the alert with all perseverance and petition for all the saints; I will pray that utterance may be given to me in the opening of my mouth to make known with boldness the mystery of the Gospel. In the name of Jesus Christ.

Ephesians 6:10-19

PSALM 91

1. Thank You Lord that I will dwell in the shelter of the Most High. I shall rest in the shadow of the Almighty.

2. I will say of the Lord, He is my refuge and fortress; my God, in whom I trust.

3. Surely He will deliver me from the snare of the fowler and from the perilous pestilence.

4. He will cover me with His feathers and in His wings I will take refuge. His truth shall be my shield and buckler.

5. I shall not be afraid of the terror by night nor the arrow that flies by day.

6. Nor the pestilence that walks in darkness nor the destruction that lays waste at noonday.

7. A thousand may fall at my side and ten thousand at my right hand, but it will not come near me.

8. Only with my eyes will I look, and see the punishment of the wicked!

9. Because I have made the Lord who is my refuge even the Most High, my dwelling place,

10. No evil shall befall me, nor shall any plague come near my dwelling.

11. For He shall give His angels charge over me to keep me in all my ways.

12. In their hands they shall bear me up lest I dash my foot against a stone.

13. I shall tread upon the lion and the cobra; the young lion and the serpent I shall trample under foot.

14. Because I have set my love upon Him, therefore He will deliver me. He will set me on high, because I have known HIS NAME.

15. I will call upon Him, and He will answer me; He will be with me in trouble; He will deliver me and honor me.

16. With long life He will satisfy me and show me HIS SALVATION.

In the name of Jesus Christ

> For if you forgive men for their transgressions, your Heavenly Father will also forgive you. But if you do not forgive men, then Your Father will not forgive your transgressions. *(The words of Jesus)*
>
> *Matthew 6:14-15*

FORGIVENESS

It is important to keep our spiritual slate clean at all times as we intercede for the needs of others. **Harboring any unforgiveness or unconfessed sins will definitely hinder prayers.** *Unforgiveness can be detrimental to our physical and spiritual well-being. It can manifest itself as depression, anger, hatred, resentment and physical ailments, all of which rob us of peace, joy, health, and power. Forgiveness and repentance bring spiritual renewal, and a fresh anointing of the Holy Spirit.*

I have a short forgiveness prayer that I composed after attending a conference on inner healing led by Francis and Judith MacNutt. When you pray this prayer of forgiveness from time to time, you will experience a fresh anointing of the Holy Spirit. Forgiveness, like repentance, is not just a one time action, it is to be ongoing if we are to be powerful in the Kingdom of God. The Forgiveness Prayer is on page 19.

Make a list of all the people and situations that have ever caused you hurt, pain, rejection, fear, loneliness, resentment, anger, jealousy, guilt, shame, dishonor. Don't forget to put your own name and God's at the top of the list. This is very important!

You may think that God would bring about adverse situations in your life as a result of some sin that you had committed. **Please be assured that God would never do this.** *However, because you hold this thought about God in your mind and heart, there is the necessity to forgive Him. Sometimes you have to forgive God for having given you the parents you were assigned.*

Quite often the person you must forgive may already be dead. These people are often the most difficult to forgive, but are the most important. There may be people or situations in your life which you may feel are **impossible** *to forgive, or ones that you simply* **refuse** *to* *forgive, or ones that you say you just **cannot** forgive since they have caused you such deep pain. Tell God this, confess your difficulty, then pray the prayer below out of obedience to Him and His Word.*

> *Unforgiveness is a doorway for satan to come in and take control of your life, and even the lives of family members. Never let your unforgiveness rob your children or their children of the 'abundant life'! Remember the sins of the fathers are passed down to the 3rd and 4th generations. See Numbers 14:18.*

Watch a miracle happen!

PERSONAL FORGIVENESS PRAYER

Father, I lift to You all these people and situations, and I forgive them for hurting me, rejecting me, never being present for me. I forgive them for making me feel so unloved, so alone, so guilty, and causing me so much pain, and for demanding too much from me.

I forgive them for making me feel shamed, resentful, jealous, and angry. (Keep naming all the things you are led to pray. God will lead you.) I also ask, Father, that You forgive them for doing these things to me and I ask that You forgive me for holding a judgment against all of them.

Father, I know You don't need forgiving, but I forgive You for allowing me to be in these situations where I received so much pain. I also forgive myself for separating myself from Your love and forgiveness in all my life situations. I ask now that You fill me with Your love for these people, and for myself, and for the Lord Jesus Christ, who I believe is Your Son, Who died for me, was resurrected for me, and lives today for me. Please fill me with Jesus' love, peace, power, joy, forgiveness, and new life in Him. Fill me with Your Holy Spirit. In the name of Jesus Christ.

Thank You Lord for setting my captive spirit free!

NATIONAL FORGIVENESS PRAYER

Thank you for joining this project to pray for forgiveness throughout our land. We are praying for forgiveness for all areas where hatred, violence, and murder abound. We know that forgiveness, throughout, will heal this nation. Just as in Rwanda when people were killing each other right and left, a woman watched her entire family chopped to death in her front yard. The hatred and bitterness followed throughout but, this one woman chose to forgive. As she forgave, forgiveness spread across the nation, and today that country of Rwanda has been healed of all un-forgiveness and hatred and it's one of the strongest nations in the world.

Also in Charleston, when the pastor forgave the man who murdered so many of his parishioners, forgiveness quieted the rebellion and anger, the protesting that was coming forth. They all turned around and went back home.

So we are praying for forgiveness according to Matthew 6:14 – 15 where the Lord says, "If you forgive people their transgressions against you, then I will forgive your transgressions. But if you do not forgive, I will not forgive you." We have been praying lately for revival, for repentance, but one of the biggest sins that we hold onto his un-forgiveness. Un-forgiveness for our neighbors, un-forgiveness where ever you look, there's un-forgiveness. So follow me in this prayer and let us forgive.

Lord, I ask You to release a spirit of grace and supplication upon this nation. I ask that You grant us grace to look upon You, the One Whom we have pierced, and Lord we thank You that all people in this nation will let all bitterness and wrath and evil speaking be put far behind them, and be kind and tenderhearted toward each other, forgiving each other just as You have forgiven us.

We praise You Lord that the black man will forgive the white man, and the white man will forgive the black man, for things not only that take place presently, but for things that went on in the past. We praise You that You will put Your love in each black man's heart for the white man, and You will put Your love in each white man's heart for the black man.

And we lift up to You Congress, the Democrats and the Republicans, let them forgive each other. And let them hunger and thirst for righteousness, and let them be filled. We praise You for that Lord. Let righteousness rule our Congress, not competitive ideals. We praise You for that Lord.

And let the women who has had an abortion forgive the doctor for performing the abortion, and forgive the nurses that assisted, and forgive the people who gathered together the body parts and sold them, freeing this woman who suffered an abortion from any depression and self-hatred. Let her forgive herself Lord, for choosing abortion. We praise You for that, and let there be no more abortion. Abortion will be a thing of the past.

Let the husband forgive the wife and the wife forgive the husband for anything that they deal with or battle with in their marriage. Let the parents forgive the children for being rebellious and let the children forgive the parents. We praise You for this Lord.

Let the soldier forgive his enemy, not only the enemy that they are warring against now, but the enemies from the past, and let it free their spirits from a desolate feeling. Lord, let the veteran forgive the government and the government turn towards and help the veterans.

Lord let us forgive the people who have worked so hard to bring down this nation, to take God out of the schools, let us forgive that person for taking God out of the nation everywhere we turn. Let all people of this nation hunger for God and as they come into forgiveness Lord, You will forgive them and take them into Your heart. Lord we praise You, we thank You, we honor You, we glorify You that we will forgive our enemies. We will forgive, Lord. We will choose forgiveness above all else.

And Lord, I do lift up Donald Trump, he has been so beat up on. I ask that you give him the courage and the strength to publicly forgive his enemies, just like the woman in Rwanda. He will forgive the worst of his enemies, and in doing so he will dissolve hatred, division, anger, and murder. Lord we ask that for all those who have been hurt by Donald Trump, you will give them grace to forgive him. We thank You Lord. We praise You for the forgiving spirit that will cover this land. We praise you, Jesus. We praise You and we honor You. Thank you, Lord.

Now ladies and gentlemen, those of you who are praying for forgiveness to move in this land, I thank you again for dedicating a few minutes, a few times a week to pray this prayer over this nation for forgiveness. We thank you and we praise you. Remember if you are so led, pass it on to friends, prayer groups, and churches.

You will find an audio version of this prayer at *www.theswordofthespiritbook.com* under "audio prayers."

PRAYER OF REPENTANCE

JESUS' FIRST WORDS WHEN HE BEGAN HIS MINISTRY: "REPENT, FOR THE KINGDOM OF HEAVEN IS NEAR."   MATTHEW 4:17
JESUS WENT INTO GALILEE, PROCLAIMING THE GOOD NEWS OF GOD. "THE TIME HAS COME," HE SAID, "REPENT AND BELIEVE IN THE GOSPEL"
                                                    MARK 1:14-15
"UNLESS YOU REPENT, YOU WILL ALL PERISH."
                                                    LUKE 13:5

Holy Lord, I know that I have sinned against You by choosing to live in a manner that is not pleasing to You. I have rebelled against You in so many ways.

You ask that we love You with all of our minds, hearts, and souls, and that we love our neighbors as ourselves. I have not done this and I ask for Your forgiveness. I have broken all or most of Your commandments during my life. I have even doubted Your very existence. I have rejected Your Word. I have turned away from Your unconditional love which You have continually offered me. I have turned my back on the poor and suffering. I have defiled my flesh and spirit by living in a manner that is an abomination to You. I have led such an ungodly life by worshiping the materialism of the secular world and, from time to time, by being involved in the occult. I not only have lived sinfully, but I either have condoned or kept silent concerning the sins of others.

Lord, I truly repent of all this sin in my life. I repent of the sins about which I know, and the sins about which I don't know. Forgive me Lord of pride, rebellion, vanity, jealousy, judging, distrust, prejudice, adultery, fornication, all sexual sins I have committed that so grieve Your heart, dishonesty, theft, murder and greed. Please forgive me for my refusal and/or inability to forgive others. Take all this sin from me, Lord. Wash me clean with the blood of Jesus Christ. Create in me a clean heart and renew a right spirit within me, a spirit that will worship You, glorify You, and serve You for the rest of my life. In the name of Jesus Christ!

Text taken from *Sword of the Spirit* by Joy Lamb 6th edition.
Used by permission of Lamb's Books, Inc. • 3368 Lakeshore Blvd. • Jacksonville, FL 32210

FREEDOM FROM GUILT

Lord, speak to me of guilt, it seems to trap so many and keep them in bondage:

'Guilt destroys the soul, for it completely negates My covenant with the people. I died on the cross for your sins and your guilt. Remember the scripture 'I will acknowledge my sin to You, and my iniquity I will not hide. I will confess my transgressions to the Lord, and the Lord will forgive the guilt of my sin' (Psalm 32:5). That is exactly what I do when you confess Me as the Son of God. If you truly accept Me and my Word and repent, you will know that and be free of all sin and guilt. You will listen to Me. You will follow My Words, those words spoken to you in quiet moments and My Words spoken to you in the Scriptures. You will hold fast to those words and nothing will cause you to doubt. Doubt brings distrust, distrust brings anguish, anguish brings fear, fear brings separation, separation brings sin, sin brings guilt, and that guilt brings sickness to the mind, body and soul. Satan is the author of sin, guilt and death. I the Lord am the author of Life. Choose Life My Child!'

SCRIPTURAL PRAYERS
FOR FREEDOM FROM GUILT

Thank You Lord that I will confess my transgressions to You, and You will forgive the guilt of my sin.

Psalm 32:5

Thank You Lord that I believe in You and from my innermost being will flow rivers of living waters.

John 7:38

O Lord I thank You that You will make those living waters flow constantly in my soul. In the name of Jesus Christ.

DELIVERANCE

As you pray for the needs of others, you are actually becoming a prayer warrior, just as Jesus was and is today, constantly interceding for us to the Father. It is written that Jesus was sent to destroy the works of the devil (I John 3:8). We are to do the same! Jesus said that greater works would we do than He did. Isn't it exciting to know we as believers have that power? All we have to do is to live into that promise of the Word. We have power over the demonic world, and all the demonic forces connected with that world. It is our duty as believing Christians, and especially as intercessors, to apply that power, and to destroy any destructive force brought about by satan. This can be done by binding and loosing in the name of Jesus Christ, and praying God's Holy Word.

You will find that as you enter into battle as a warrior, satan will no doubt plan a counter attack. Therefore, it is wise to stay on the alert and remember the Deliverance Prayer, a mighty tool for keeping satan at bay. Praying the Deliverance Prayer over yourself and your family may seem a tedious burden at first, but as you experience the power of this prayer, you will respect its part in intercession. Putting on the full armor of God is also a wonderful weapon against the powers of satan. The most powerful weapon of all against satan is God's Holy Word. No power of darkness can stand against the Word of God!

For a more in-depth understanding of deliverance and how to deal with the evil that seems to have a grip on today's world, I would like to recommend Deliverance From Evil Spirits. A Practical Manual *by Dr. Francis MacNutt.*

This book is available in most Christian Bookstores. You may order one directly from Christian Healing Ministries at www.christianhealingmin.org or 904-765-3332 extension 219.

PRAYER OF PROTECTION/DELIVERANCE

In the name of Jesus Christ I present to You Father, myself, my family, and all my relationships, my home and property, my possessions, my finances, and my health. I lift to You all families, all churches, and all facets of the U.S. government, all forms of the media and all entertainment industries, all electronic communication devices, all health institutions. I lift to You all Nations' economies (especially the U.S. Economy), all schools and all universities, all neighborhoods, all land, towns and cities in America, and all nations of the world, and each person and area for whom and which I am praying. I also lift to You, Lord, every church leader, Christian organization, and all Intercessors in America and all nations of the world. I lift to You Lord, *The Sword Of the Spirit the Word of God* and *Families and Churches United in Word Prayer for the Freedom and Healing of America*. By the power and authority of the name of Jesus Christ, through HIS shed blood and the Holy Word of God, I rebuke you satan and all the dominions of darkness and all infiltrations and activities of the angel of light and all demonic assignments seeking entrance into my life and the lives of the people, areas, and situations for whom and for which I am praying. **"For this reason was the Son of God made manifest to destroy the works of the devil! In the name of Jesus Christ."** (1John 3:8).

In the name of Jesus Christ I command that the ways and works of darkness over all of us and all the people in America to be broken! I rebuke the satanic forces of nature from harming any property that we possess and any area for which I am praying in the name of Jesus Christ. In the name of Jesus Christ, Father, I ask You to send the presence and power of Your Holy Spirit and Your Holy Angels to drive the devil far from me and each person, group, and area for whom and for which I am praying, and to cleanse every place where the enemy has gained a foothold. Holy Spirit, come and manifest as a cleansing fire. In the name of Jesus Christ.

In the name of Jesus I resist and break all curses, hexes, spells, Voodoo, fasting prayers (not of the Lord), all satanic and masonic rituals, the power of all blood sacrifices and covenants, any and all witchcraft and sorcery sent against any of us, or any area, or transferred through the generational bloodline. In the name of Jesus Christ I apply the blood of Jesus Christ to break all strongholds of iniquity and rebellion in myself and all the people that I have lifted to You this day. Lord, in the name of Jesus Christ, I ask You to expose and bring into the light negative inner vows and strongholds that contradict Your Word and Your Will. By the breath of Your Spirit, release Your truth as a Sword and Your Word to expose falsehood curses of self rejection, self-hatred, and reactive hatred and bitterness towards others. I take up the Sword of Your Word and cut myself and each person for whom I am praying this day, free from death, hell, destruction, violence and murder! I also cut us free from the bondage of all generational demonic forces of resentment, low self-esteem, insecurity, division, infirmity, procrastination, exhaustion, anger, the occult, depression, oppression, memory loss, perversion, incest, homosexuality, adultery, fornication, abortion, lust, the antichrist's demonic spiritual forces of control, distrust, fear, bitterness, pride, vanity, jealousy, rebellion, competitiveness, busyness, manipulation, dishonesty, deception-lying tongue, inferiority, political correctness, lawlessness, mind control, self pity, rejection, grudge bearing, anxiety, stress, confusion, greed, envy, kleptomania, theft and "blindness," resentment, guilt, unforgiveness, defiance, and ungodly character defects, drug addictions, alcohol abuse, gluttony, all body piercing, harassing spirits, controlling spirits of Jezebel and Ahab, religious spirits, and the spirit of separation between families and races. In the name of Jesus Christ I renounce all relationships dishonoring to the Lord in my life and the lives of the people I have lifted to You, Lord, this day! In the name of Jesus Christ, I break the power of soul ties over our minds and our emotions. I proclaim my and their freedom to become children of Yahweh God, to live as He intended us to live, filled and overflowing with the life and the power of His Holy Spirit, filled with the light and love of Jesus Christ. I claim the full protection of the shed blood of Jesus Christ, the Son of the Living God over all of our lives, our marriages, our relationships, our families, our possessions, our churches, our neighborhoods, our towns, our nation and for all the people, areas, and situations that I have lifted to You, Lord, this day. You, Lord, are a shield about us, our glory and the lifter of our heads. (Psalm 3:3) Blessed be the name of the Lord. In the name of Jesus Christ!

Thank You Lord that You will awaken our sleeping spirits and bring us into the light. Thank You Lord that You will transform us by the renewing of our minds daily in Christ Jesus. Thank You Lord that You will pour out Your Spirit on us, and reveal Your Word to us. In the name of Jesus Christ. Thank You Lord that You will give Your angels charge over all of us in all of our ways. Thank You Lord that we believe in You and from our innermost being shall flow Rivers of Living Waters. Thank You Lord that You will direct our hearts into the love of God and the steadfastness of Jesus Christ. In the name of Jesus Christ. Thank You Lord that we will all hunger and thirst for righteousness and we will all be filled. In the name of Jesus Christ

Thank You Lord that You will heal us and we will be healed. In the name of Jesus Christ. Thank You Lord that no weapon formed against our spiritual, physical, and mental beings shall ever prosper. In the name of Jesus Christ.

Thank You Lord that you will say to satan, "the Lord rebuke you satan! The Lord who has chosen Jerusalem" rebuke you in all the lives, situations, and areas, I just lifted to the Lord! In the name of Jesus Christ!!!

Zechariah 3:2

GOD IS GOD

Oh Lord thank You, thank You, that You answer me, so that all the people and organizations that I just lifted to You will know that You are God, and You are turning all hearts in America back to You. In the name of Jesus Christ!!!

1 Kings :18:37

Thank You Lord that satan will have no dominion over any person, group, organization, area, or situation that I lifted to You this day, because You are You. God is God! In the name of Jesus Christ.

Thank You Lord that from heaven, Your dwelling place, You will hear our prayers and our pleas, and uphold our cause. And forgive Your people, who have sinned against You. In the name of Jesus Christ.

1 Kings 8:49

Thank You Lord that all the people I lifted to You this day will be devoted to prayer and ministry of The Word. In the name of Jesus Christ.

Acts 6:4

Now Lord I cut myself free from all intercession. I lay my prayers at Your feet, knowing that You have heard my prayers and You will answer these prayers, and You will accomplish all that concerns me. In the name of Jesus Christ. I plead the blood of Jesus Christ over all that I have lifted to You this day for Your divine protection. Thank You Lord that You will protect us and our families and America by the Power of Your mighty name and Your blood, the blood of Jesus Christ! In the name of Jesus Christ.

SHATTERING YOUR STRONGHOLDS PRAYER

I have included a prayer from Shattering Your Strongholds *by Rev. Liberty S. Savard.* This prayer stresses the importance of binding ourselves and others to the will and purposes of God and loosing the strongholds from our souls that prevent healing prayers from penetrating our spirits. I recommend that you incorporate this powerful prayer into your deliverance intercession.* Shattering Your Strongholds *is excellent reading for all involved in intercession, whether individual or corporate.*

In the name of Jesus Christ, I bind _____'s body, soul and spirit to the will and purposes of God for his/her life. I bind _____'s mind, will and emotions to the will of God. I bind him/her to the truth and to the blood of Jesus. I bind his/her mind to the mind of Christ, that the very thoughts, feelings and purposes of His heart would be within his/her thoughts. I bind _____'s feet to the paths of righteousness that his/her steps would be steady and sure. I bind him/her to the work of the cross with all of its mercy, grace, love, forgiveness and dying to self.

I loose every old, wrong, ungodly pattern of thinking, attitude, idea, desire, belief, motivation, and every wrong mind/body agreement he/she has about wrong behaviors. I tear down, crush, smash and destroy every stronghold associated with these things. I loose any stronghold in his/ her life that has been justifying and protecting hard feelings against anyone. I loose the strongholds of unforgiveness, fear, and distrust from him/her.

"I loose the power and effects of wrong agreements from _____. I loose deceptions and lies from _____'s mind, and I loose the effects and influences of any soul ties he/she has with other people. I loose the confusion and blindness from the god of this world from _____'s mind that has kept him/her from seeing the light of the gospel of Jesus Christ. I call forth every precious word of Scripture that has ever entered into his/her mind and heart that it would rise up in power within him/her.

"In the name of Jesus, I loose the power and effects of any harsh or hard words (word curses) spoken to, about or by _____. I loose all generational bondage, thinking and associated strongholds from _____. I loose all grave clothes from him/her. I loose all effects and bondages from him/her that may have been caused by mistakes I have made.

"Father, in the name of Jesus, I crush, smash and destroy generational bondages of any kind from mistakes made at any point between generations. I destroy them right here, right now. They will not bind and curse any more members of this family. I bind and loose these things in Jesus's name. He has given me the keys and the authority to do so. Thank You Lord for the truth. Amen."

*Used by permission of Rev. Liberty Savard, Pres., Liberty Savard Ministries,
P.O. Box 41260, Sacramento CA 95841 1993 Bridge-Logos Publishers, New Brunswick, NJ

May we all be loosed from the strongholds of anger, anxiety, competition, confusion, control, deceit, denial, depression, disease, disobedience, distress, distrust, doubt, envy, false security, fear, fornication, gossip, greed, guilt, hostility, immorality, immaturity, independence of God, isolation, jealousy, lust, manipulation, oppression, prejudice, pride, rebellion, self indulgence, sickness, suppression, violence and wickedness, procrastination, sibling rivalry, people pleasing attributes and intimidation.

CUTTING FREE PRAYER
FOLLOWING INTERCESSION

Lord Jesus, thank You for sharing with me/us Your wonderful ministry of healing and deliverance. Thank You for the healing I/we have seen and experienced today, but I/we realize that the sickness and evil we encounter is more than our humanity can bear, so cleanse me/us of any sadness, and negative thinking or despair that I/we may have picked up during intercession for others.

If my/our ministry has tempted me/us to anger, impatience or lust, cleanse me/us of those temptations, and replace them with love, joy, and peace. If any evil spirits have attached themselves to me or oppressed me in any way, I command you, spirits of earth, air, fire, or water, or of the netherworld or of nature to depart now and go straight to Jesus Christ, for Him to deal with as He will.

Come Holy Spirit, renew me, fill me anew with Your power, Your life, and Your joy. Strengthen me where I have felt weak and clothe me with Your light. Fill me with Your life.

Lord Jesus, please send Your holy angels to minister to me/us and protect me/us and my family, from all sickness, harm, and accidents, and give us safe travel. We praise You now and forever, Father, Son, and Holy Spirit!

By Francis MacNutt used by permission

Now my God may Your eyes be open and Your ears attentive to the prayers in this place. In the Name of Jesus Christ.

II Chronicles 6:40

A PRAYER TO BREAK ANY CURSE THAT MAY HAVE BEEN PLACED ON YOU

Lord Jesus Christ, I believe that You are the Son of God; and the only way to God, and that You died on the cross for my sins, and rose again from the dead.

I give up all my rebellion, and all my sin, and I submit myself to You as my Lord.

I confess all my sins before You, and ask for Your forgiveness – especially for any sins that have exposed me to a curse. Release me from the consequences of my ancestors' sins.

By a decision of my will, I forgive all who have harmed me or wronged me–just as I want God to forgive me. In particular, I forgive _____.

I renounce all contact with anything occult or satanic – if I have any 'contact' objects, charms, games, artifacts and books, I commit myself to destroy them. I cancel all satan's claims against me.

Lord Jesus, I believe that on the cross You took on Yourself every curse that could ever come upon me. So I ask You now to release me from every curse over my life, in Your name, Lord Jesus Christ!

From *Blessings and Curse: You Can Choose* by Derek Prince used by permission

PRAYER OF SALVATION

1.   Heavenly Father I want to be saved and come into the fullness of You. I know that I have sinned in my life, and I ask that you forgive all my sins, the ones I know about and the ones I don't know about. I now confess with my mouth that Jesus Christ IS the Son of God, and I believe in my heart that God raised Him from the dead. I ask that Jesus Christ come into my heart and create in me the kind of person You, Father, had intended me to be from the moment of my conception. I thank You for this wonderful gift, and now I know that I am saved. Thank You Lord for transforming me through the renewing of my mind through Christ Jesus. In the name of Jesus Christ.

2.   Lord Jesus Christ,

   I am sorry for the things I have done wrong in my life. (Take a few moments to ask His forgiveness for anything particular that is on your conscience.) Please forgive me. I now turn from everything which I know is wrong.

   Thank you that you died on the cross for me so that I could be forgiven and set free. Thank you that you offer me forgiveness and the gift of your Spirit. I now receive that gift. Please come into my life by your Holy Spirit to be with me forever.

   Thank you, Lord Jesus. Amen

From *Why Jesus?*
by Nicky Gumbel used by permission

RENOUNCING THE OCCULT

Heavenly Father, in the name of Jesus Christ, I renounce satan and all his works, witchcraft, the use of divination, practicing of sorcery, dealings with mediums and spiritualists, ouija boards, astrology, horoscopes, numerology, all types of fortune-telling cards, palm reading, tea-leaves reading, levitation, and anything associated with the occult and satan; I renounce all of them, and I will never go back to them again. In the name of the Lord Jesus Christ. In the name of Jesus Christ, I now take the Sword of the Spirit and cut myself and the present generation of my family free from the effects of occult contamination in previous generations. All effects from contact with evil that have filtered through my family line must now cease. I ask the Holy Spirit to come and fill all those areas with His love, joy, peace, and His Spirit. In the name of Jesus Christ.

2 Kings 21:6, 2 Chronicles 33:6, Deuteronomy 18:9-13

RECEIVING THE BAPTISM
OF THE HOLY SPIRIT

Dear Lord Jesus Christ, thank You for the most exciting gift on earth, the gift of salvation, but Lord Jesus, You promised us another gift, the gift of the Holy Spirit. So I ask You, Lord Jesus, to baptize me in and with the Holy Spirit, just as You baptized Your disciples on the day of Pentecost.

I want to be a disciple of Yours, Lord, filled with the Holy Spirit just as Your disciples were. I will try to do what You tell me to do. I forgive all those who have ever caused me pain, harm, rejection, or shame, and I ask You to forgive them. I also ask that You forgive me for holding a judgment against them. Breathe on me Your Holy Spirit. Thank You Lord, for hearing my prayer. I will lift up my hands unto the Lord worshiping You and praising You with all my heart in the Spirit, giving thanks, praise and glory to You forever. In the name of Jesus Christ.

Thank You Lord that You would grant to all of us according to the riches of Your glory to be strengthened with power through Your Holy Spirit in our inner man, so that Christ may dwell in our hearts, through faith, and that we, being rooted and grounded in love, may be able to comprehend with all the saints what is the breadth and length and height and depth and to know the love of Christ which surpasses knowledge, that we may be filled up to all the fullness of God. In the name of Jesus Christ.

Ephesians 3:16-19

A NEED TO BE FREE
THE CONSEQUENCES OF FREEMASONRY
INVOLVEMENT

by Francis MacNutt

Many people in our country, including ministers, have been involved in Freemasonry. Many who come to CHM for prayer have been involved directly, and even more have Masonic influences in their ancestry. Scholarly books have been written on the history of the Masonic rites, so this is a brief account of why people need to be cut free from the harmful effects of Masonry.

First, it should be said that many enter a Lodge for reasons of business and to join an association of friends upon whom they can rely. Many of the Presidents of the United States, including George Washington, were Masons and the back of our dollar bill is filled with Masonic symbols (such as the all-seeing eye of the Grand Architect of the Universe). My great-uncle, Francis A. MacNutt, who was in the U.S. diplomatic service, was told by the Secretary of State that he would not advance in the service unless he became a Mason. He refused and left the diplomatic service.

Moreover, the early history of the Masons set them in opposition to organized churches, Catholicism in particular, and the Masons were responsible for various religious persecutions (in the 18th Century, for example, the Jesuits were suppressed in several countries). The opposition was so strong that Catholics were forbidden to join the Masons.

The second reason that Christians have traditionally been against Masonry is that the Church has been against societies that take oaths of secrecy, with dire threats of evil (death) that are incurred for violating the curse. "If you have read any of the initiation rites of the various levels all the way up to the 33rd Degree, you realize that they appeal to fear at a very deep level (at one level, a noose is placed around your neck).

The most important factor, though, is that false gods, replacing Jesus Christ, are invoked. For example, the Egyptian gods, Horus, Set, and Isis are invoked at the 31st Degree. With each degree, the confusion and idolatry increase, until Lucifer himself becomes part of the initiation. The sin involved in Masonry is ultimately idolatry and involves the rejection of Jesus Christ as our only savior.

For this reason, if we ourselves have been part of the Masonic religion, *we need to repent and to renounce our involvement at each of the levels in which we have taken part*. Prayer for deliverance from the effects of Masonry may also be needed. If these prayers seem slow in taking effect, we encourage you to read about the various levels of initiation and their effects so you can pray in greater depth for the effects of masonry on your life. Some people are freed by a relatively simple prayer, but others need more depth. Prayers will be needed, too, to release you from generational curses which you, your family, or your ancestors may have incurred.

In addition to men's organizations associated with the Masons, such as the Shriners, women also take part through groups such as the Eastern Star and the Rainbow Girls; and for boys, there is the Order of De Molay. Entire areas of our country where masonry has been dominant (such as Richmond, Virginia) seem to be resistant to fervent Christianity.

In general, because Masons do so much good work (Shriners' hospitals and circuses), most Christians find it hard to believe that there are any real dangers connected with being a Mason, especially since many seem to join for mainly social or business reasons.

If you want to become more fully informed about the Masons, we encourage you to read books such as *Christianity and American Freemasonry* by William Whalen, and *Masonry Unmasked* by John Salza.

by Francis MacNutt used by permission.

None of these writings are meant to offend any Mason, family member or friend of a Mason. They are given for his protection from the consequences of involvement in Freemasonry. "My people perish for lack of knowledge". I am sure that no Christian or Jewish believer would intentionally rebel against God by becoming or remaining a Mason if they believe God is Who He says He is.

These men usually join the brotherhood for fellowship or to implant themselves in the business or political community for recognition and advancement. However, because of the vows spoken in each level or degree of the Freemasonry initiation ceremonies, they have rebelled against God simply by calling on other gods to strengthen their commitment. It is at this point that they open themselves and family members or generations to a curse. The important thing to understand is that this curse will not only come upon them, but will be passed down to future generations.

"Therefore I will bring charges against you again declares the Lord. And I will bring charges against your children's children.

Jeremiah 3:24

They have knowingly or unknowingly broken two of the Ten Commandments: You shall have no other Gods before Me. You shall not make for yourself an idol in the form of anything in heaven above or on the earth beneath or in the waters below. You shall not bow down to them or worship them: for I, the Lord your God, am a jealous God punishing the children for the sin of the fathers to the third and forth generation of those who hate me, but showing love to a thousand generations of those who love me and keep my commandments.

Some of these curses can manifest in different ways. The intercessors/prayer counselors at Christian Healing Ministries have ministered to many people with a multitude of problems. Some of these problems can be traced to their involvement or a family member's involvement in Freemasonry. Some of the manifestations of these problems are the inability to conceive, or the inability to carry a child full term, or miscarriages: insufficient funds for life needs, unsettling or hostile relationships in marriages or family relationships, especially sibling relationships, addiction of all kinds especially alcoholism and drug addiction, all kind of diseases, both mental and physical. Heart disease and especially heart attacks seem to dominate in the Freemasonry family, perhaps this is the reason for early deaths for males. Death wishes which involve suicide, bulimia or anorexia can be connected to Freemasonry. Early deaths of males and possibly their firstborns are prevalent. Lack of or weak belief in Jesus Christ as the true Son of God is also a tell-tale sign. The Lord wants these people set free to come into the knowledge of the truth, and the way to this truth is through repentance and forgiveness. Therefore they are led in a prayer of repentance and forgiveness (forgiving themselves, or the family member who was involved), and asking God to forgive them for all involvement in Freemasonry. Then they are reconciled to God.

Repentance and forgiveness are the antidotes for all sin, for repentance truly reconciles us to God. Jesus' words throughout the New Testament are repent-repent-repent! In Mark 1:14-15 Jesus state: "Repent and believe in the Gospel!" One must realize that the Gospel during Jesus' walk on earth was every word of the OLD TESTAMENT. Jesus also states the "Scripture cannot be broken" John 10:35. Read Deuteronomy chapter 28. This chapter in the Bible clearly explains the blessings of obedience and the consequences of disobedience, which is rebellion, and we know who the author of rebellion is. Blessings or Curses, you can choose!!!

May the Lord bless all of you who read this text and participate in being set free through the following prayers, and may our Lord give you a deeper understanding of the Scriptures. May the Holy Spirit open your minds to understand Scripture.

Joy Lamb

PRAYER OF RELEASE FROM THE CURSES OF FREEMASONRY

- Introductory comment and prayer of renunciation of Freemasonry by William Schnoebelen, a former Mason: "If you are a Mason, you need to pray a prayer of repentance, renouncing the Lodge. You may wish to pray it with a friend or your pastor, although this is by no means essential... Just pray with all your heart. You should pray something like this:

- "In the name of the Lord Jesus Christ and by the authority I possess as a believer in Him, I declare that I am redeemed out of the hand of the devil. Through the blood of Jesus, all my sins are forgiven. The blood of Jesus Christ, God's Son, is cleansing me now from all sin. Through it I am righteous, just as if I had never sinned.

- "Through the blood of Jesus, I am sanctified, made holy, set apart for God – for I am a member of a chosen generation, a royal priesthood, a holy nation, a peculiar people; that I should show forth Your praises, Lord God, Who has called me out of darkness into Your marvelous light (1 Pet. 2:9). My body is a temple for the Holy Spirit, redeemed, and cleansed by the blood of Jesus.

- "I belong to the Lord Jesus Christ, body, soul and spirit. His blood protects me from all evil. In Jesus' name, I confess right now that I have been guilty of the sin of idolatry in the Masonic Lodge (1 John 1:9). In agreement with the Lord, I call that involvement sin, and ask Him to completely remove it from my life and the lives of my family.

- "In the name of Jesus, I rebuke any and all the lying and deceitful spirits of Freemasonry which may think that they still have a claim on me or my family (James 4:7). In Jesus' name, I renounce the spirits of Freemasonry, Ba'al, Jahbalon, Baphomet and Tubalcain, and declare that you have no power over me anymore, for I am bought and paid for by the blood of Jesus, shed on Calvary.

- "I renounce any and all oaths made at the altar of Freemasonry in Jesus' holy name; and by the power of his shed blood I also break any generational sin and bondage which may be oppressing me through oaths made by my parents or ancestors (Exodus 20:5), and I nail all these things to the cross of Christ (Colossians 2:14).

- "I also break any and all power of the devil through these oaths over my own children or grandchildren and command him to leave them alone, for they are under the blood of the Lamb of God! I also ask the Lord to cleanse any possible sin of illegitimacy through the tenth generation with the blood of Jesus (Deuteronomy 23:2).

- "Because of the blood of Jesus, Satan has no more power over me or my family, and no place in us. I renounce him and his hosts completely and declare them to be my enemies.

- "Jesus said: 'These signs shall follow them that believe; in My name shall they cast out devils (Mark 16:17).' I am a believer, and in the name of Jesus I exercise my authority and expel all evil spirits. I command them to leave me now, according to the Word of God and in the name of Jesus. 'Forgetting those things which are behind, and reaching forth unto those things which are before, I press toward the mark for the prize of the high calling of God in Christ Jesus (Philippians 3:13·14).' In Jesus name. Amen."

This prayer taken from the book Masonry Beyond the Light *by William Schnoebelen. Pages 266-268. Prayer used by permission. Mr Schnoebelen's website for his ministry dealing with Free Masonry is www.withoneaccord. org.*

Note: Selwyn Stevens, noted Christian author and speaker, offers a prayer on his website (JubileeResourcesUSA) that addresses the sins of each level of Freemasonry in greater detail. www.jubileeresources.org

PRAYER FOR THE HEALING OF UNHEALTHY EFFECTS OF CONCEPTION

Heavenly Father, Creator of everything that lives, my Creator, go back to my very beginning. Release me from any harmful effects stemming from my conception, and anything wrong in my parents' relationship. Fill the moment of my conception with all the love and joy that You always wanted me to have. I know that You desired and planned my life with an everlasting love, stretching back to the very beginning of the world. Please let me know this in the very depths of my heart. Let me know how much You longed for me. In place of the darkness in my heart, fill me with Your light and love. Free me from every feeling of rejection and worthlessness. Let me know beyond the shadow of a doubt that I am Your child. Fill me with all the mother's and father's love that I so needed and missed. Let the very moment when I came to life be filled with Your light and love. In the name of Jesus Christ.

PRAYER FOR FREEING YOUR CHILD FROM HEREDITARY PREDISPOSITION TO SICKNESS

Jesus, You know my family has a predisposition to (identify the weakness). We ask You to break this weakness and free our child, in Your name. By the sword of the Spirit, let our child be set free from any weakness or inclination to (name weakness). Let our child be set free at any level this weakness exists, whether it be spiritual or physical. If there is any demonic force that influences this sickness, we bind up that evil force in Your name. And now we command you, spirit of infirmity (or addiction), to leave our child and go straight to Jesus for Him to deal with, as He will! And now, Lord Jesus, fill our child with Your health, Your love and power to replace any weakness that may have been there. Enable our child to embrace life. And we thank You, Lord Jesus, that this is being done. In the name of Jesus Christ.

From *Praying for your Unborn Child* by Francis MacNutt used by permission

PRAYER FOR HEALING FOR THOSE WHO HAVE HAD MISCARRIAGES OR ABORTIONS

Having a miscarriage or abortion can traumatize the human spirit in such a way that the pain of the trauma or "wounded spirit" can be passed on to future generations. Confession, repentance and receiving the forgiveness and grace of our dear Lord Jesus Christ can bring new life and freedom to both the mother and father, even when the parents of the aborted or miscarried child are not married to each other. Understand that repentance is not necessary when the woman has had a miscarriage other than repentance for the guilt she may hold.

The second aspect of the healing is naming the child and committing the child to the Lord Jesus Christ, and asking the Lord to receive the unborn baby into His Kingdom. You will be amazed after praying this prayer. The captive spirit is truly set free.

For the mother or father of the aborted child pray:

"Father, I repent of having an abortion. I know I have sinned against You, myself and my unborn child and I truly repent and ask for Your forgiveness. I want to name my baby. His/her name is _____, I ask that you bless and receive _____ into Your Kingdom in the name of Jesus Christ. Thank You Lord for forgiving the guilt of my sin. In the name of Jesus Christ. Thank You Lord for setting my captive spirit free. In the name of Jesus Christ.

For the parents of the miscarried child: Lord, I want to name my child and I want to commit my child to You and ask that You receive _____ into Your Kingdom. I ask, Lord, that You free me from all guilt, shame, pain and grief connected to this miscarriage. Lord, if this miscarriage is a result of sin in my life or the lives of past generations that have resulted in a curse on my being, I sincerely repent of the sin and ask You to break the curse or curses that have come on me or have been passed down from past generational sin. Lord I ask that the curses be broken and never go forth from this time forward. In the name of Jesus Christ.

Exodus 23:25-27

PRAYER FOR SEXUALLY ABUSED AND INCEST SURVIVOR'S PRAYER

We have had several incest survival victims and sexual abuse victims contact us asking for prayer because of the innumerable ongoing issues they are suffering. Praying the Deliverance Scriptures, Inner Healing Scriptures and the Deliverance Prayer have given relief to many. (See Answered Prayers under 'Deliverance' in the back of the book, page 184). However, in-depth prayer ministry is almost always a necessity for the Lord to bring someone who has suffered this type of wounding into complete freedom. Below is a prayer written by a sexually abused and incest survivor which, prayed along with the prayers mentioned above, has been very helpful for her and other survivors during recovery.

God, My Father, Lord Jesus, my Savior and Redeemer, Holy Spirit, my Comforter, my name is _____, You know me well, and for that I thank You. I praise You, I love You. I exalt Your Holy Name. I thank You that Your will is being done on this earth.

I ask for myself, and other sexually abused incest survivors, Your protection, fearlessness, tenacity, and empowerment to keep seeking Your truth, Your goodness, Your guidance to help us to think rightly and clearly, and to keep on keeping on in truth, even though it hurts deeply. You, Christ Jesus, died and rose again for us desecrated human beings so that we could come into Your presence. Let us be given Your Holy boldness to keep coming toward Your light. Help us to not allow ourselves to be turned away, or to fall away, because we think our sinfulness is greater and deeper, because it is our sexuality that was perverted at such an early age. Help us to know the sin done against us was not our fault. Help us to understand that as soon as we can work through the pain and rage of our lives, You will give us new lives.

Give us the courage to face our own sinfulness, which we have allowed to grow out of the evil done against us. You and only You can understand how twisted we are because of the sins done against us. You and only You can deliver us and cause Your light to shine on and through us.

Thank You Jesus, our best Friend, with our best interest first place in Your heart. Thank You Jesus that You are able to love each one of us best, and that You and You alone understand how much we desperately need kind care and attention. Thank You that through the Holy Spirit You can come to us and cause us to know You intimately as no other person can or will, not even ourselves. Bless You Almighty God. In the name of Jesus Christ.

Lord I forgive the person/persons that abused me. I forgive them totally and completely for causing me such anguish all these years. Lord I ask that You forgive these tormented souls. Set us all free Lord. Set us free. In the name of Jesus Christ.

By Pat Zink used by permission

✳ ✳ ✳

Teenagers and the youth of today are the Christians Leaders of tomorrow. Their sanctification and transformation through knowing Jesus is crucial to the survival of Christianity and bringing others to Jesus in the coming years. I met a wonderful Christian youth counselor via a phone conversation when she was ordering **The Sword of the Spirit** *for a youth conference. The conversation led me to incorporate prayers for teenagers and the "younger generation." Prayers that would set them free to live the abundant life of love, truth, peace, joy, and confidence, and to go forth to do the Lord's will. Thank you for your contribution to this edition of* **The Sword of the Spirit!**

PRAYERS FOR TEENAGERS AND THE YOUTH OF THE NATION

PRAYER FOR TEENAGER'S FAMILY

Lord Jesus, I forgive my family. Specifically I forgive my mother, father, brothers, sisters and any and all members of my family for hurting me. I forgive them for not loving themselves, each other or me in a manner pleasing to you Jesus, or to me.

Please heal (names) _____from the brokenness that we have experienced. Please make our hearts whole in You Lord. Help us reconcile with each other and with You Jesus. Help us find peace in You. I trust You Jesus, in this process, and I pray for Your patience and truth to fill my heart.

Please show my family and me, Your way Jesus to an abundant life here on earth and in heaven. Provide me with the love of a mother, father, sister, and brother so that I may know that love, and be able to pass it on to others.

Thank You Lord that You tell us if we claim to be without sin, we deceive ourselves and the truth is not in us. If we confess our sins, You are faithful and just and will forgive us our sins and purify us from all unrighteousness. In the name of Jesus Christ.

1 John 1:8-9

Thank You Lord that if I forgive people for their transgressions toward me, You will forgive me, but if I do not forgive people, then YOU will not forgive my transgressions. In the name of Jesus Christ.

Matthew 6:14-15

(See Forgiveness Prayer pages 18-19)

Thank You Lord that we will not let anyone lead us astray. Thank You that You tell us, "He who does what is right is righteous, just as You are righteous." In the name of Jesus Christ.

1 John 3:7

Thank You Lord that if I remain in You and Your Words remain in me, I can ask whatever I wish, and it will be given me. Thank You that this is to Your Father's glory that I bear much fruit, showing myself to be Your disciple. In the name of Jesus Christ.

John 15:7-8

TEENAGE DELIVERANCE PRAYER

Lord Jesus, please forgive me and deliver me and the young adults of our Nation from depression, anger, bitterness, lust, premarital sex, laziness, self-hatred, self-rejection, suicidal thoughts and suicidal attempts, cheating, lying, stealing, gossiping, fear, guilt, cutting ourselves, piercing, tattooing, anxiety, pornography, new age, idolatry, rebellion, materialism, violent movies, video games, books, reading material of false doctrine and the occult, promoting death, destruction, witchcraft, anorexia, and bulimia. In the name of Jesus Christ.

(Please see Deliverance Prayer page 25 and
Prayer of Repentance page 22)

Thank You Lord that The Spirit of the Sovereign LORD is on me/us, because the LORD had anointed me/us to preach good news to the poor. He has sent me/us to bind up the brokenhearted, to proclaim freedom for the captives and release from darkness for the prisoners. In the name of Jesus Christ.

Isaiah 61:1-3

Thank You Lord that the wolf will live with the lamb, the leopard will lie down with the goat, the calf and the lion and the yearling together; and a little child will lead them. In the name of Jesus Christ.
Isaiah 11:6

WHO I AM IN CHRIST PRAYER

Lord Jesus, thank you that I am more than a conqueror through Christ Jesus. Thank you Lord that I can do all things through Christ Jesus who strengthens me. Help me walk as a child of God, not of this world. May the righteousness of God pour out of my heart, into every aspect of my life. I know that You love me Jesus, thank You for dying on the cross for me. I trust You Jesus, and my heart belongs to You. I am a child of The Living God!!! In the name of Jesus Christ.

Thank You Lord that as the Father has loved You, so have You loved me. Now I will remain in Your love. If I obey Your commands, I will remain in Your love, just as You have obeyed Your Father's commands and remain in His love. In the name of Jesus Christ.
John 15:9-10

Thank You Lord that I did not choose You, but You chose me and appointed me to go and bear fruit – fruit that will last. Then the Father will give me whatever I ask in Your name. This is YOUR command: Love each other. In the Name of Jesus Christ

John 15:16-17

(Please see Ten Commandments page 138)

YOUTH AUTHORITY PRAYER

(Good Prayer for teachers, coaches, people in authority over youth)

Lord Jesus, I trust You with the people in authority over me in this world. Specifically, I pray for my teachers, coaches, pastors, and other leaders. I pray that they would come to a knowledge of You Jesus. May my life bring Your light Jesus, into their lives, in a manner that they would understand. May our relationship be a positive influence in both of our lives.

I thank You Lord that no weapon forged against me or my life will prosper. I know that He that is in me is greater than he that is in the world. Please give me the wisdom to resist the devil. God, please give me the eyes to see and the ears to hear and a heart that understands what You are doing in my life. Thank You Lord Jesus.

Thank You Lord that I will see with my eyes, hear with my ears, understand with my heart, return and You will heal me. In the name of Jesus Christ.

Acts 28:27

Thank You Lord that You will constantly protect me from the evils of peer pressure in thought, mind and deed. Thank You Lord that we will obey God rather than men. In the name of Jesus Christ.

Acts 5:29

Thank You Lord that You will give me understanding in everything. In the name of Jesus Christ.

2 Timothy 2:7

Thank you Lord Jesus that you have written in your word that if I bless Israel I will be blessed, and if I curse Israel I will be cursed.

Teach me to daily bless Israel in my thoughts, words, deeds, and giving, so that along with all the peoples of the earth who bless Israel, I will be blessed.

Genesis 12:3

Please note Freedom From Guilt Prayer on page 23. Many times as individuals we carry guilt left over from early childhood when harsh words were spoken to us, "shattering our young fragile spirits." As a result, we are frozen in a poor self image state and the inability to become all the Lord wants us to be. We just never felt worthy and could not understand why this was happening to us. Let God free you, He will. Pray the prayer!

Thank You Lord that You know the plans You have for me/ us, plans to prosper me/us and not to harm me/us, plans to give me/us hope and a future. In the Name of Jesus Christ.

Jeremiah 29:11

TEENAGE TESTIMONIES

I have really enjoyed praying with The Sword of the Spirit. I know it helps me pray with power. I really like the Deliverance Prayer, because it guides me to pray about things that I would not even think about praying. I never really knew how to put on the Full Armor Of God. Now I know, I am following God's plan and promises for my heart and mind when I pray that prayer and the others. I have really learned a lot about the importance of praying God's Word and promises! My Grandpa has cancer, and I used The Sword of The Spirit and he is getting better. I like the cutting free prayer, it helps me turn all of my concerns over to God.

The Sword of The Spirit has given me the ability to pray with purpose and with power. This book has helped me positively effect peoples lives with prayer. My spirit feels free after I pray these prayers, especially the Deliverance Prayer and Cutting Free Prayer. I give these books out to a lot of my friends. My friend had depression, and shortly after praying these prayers, the depression lifted. Now, she is free and happy! My confidence in the Lord has really increased, because I know I am putting on The Full Armor of God correctly. It is a great feeling!

THE CHURCH

The Commission of the Church
According to the Word of God

It is written that Jesus said to them, 'These are My words which I spoke to you while I was still with you, that all things which are written about Me in the Law of Moses and the Prophets and the Psalms must be fulfilled.' Then He opened their minds to understand the Scriptures, and He said to them, **'Thus it is written,** that the Christ should suffer and rise again from the dead the third day; and **that repentance for forgiveness of sins should be proclaimed in His name to all the nations, beginning from Jerusalem.** You are witnesses of these things. And behold I am sending forth the promise of My Father upon you; but you are to stay in the city until you are clothed with power from on high.'

Luke 24:44-49

It is written that Jesus said to them, 'Go into all the world and preach the gospel to all creation. He who has believed and has been baptized shall be saved: but he who has disbelieved shall be condemned. And these signs will accompany those who have believed in My name: they will cast out demons, they will speak with other tongues; they will pick up serpents, and if they drink any deadly poison it shall not hurt them; they will lay hands on the sick, and they will recover.'

So then, when the Lord Jesus had spoken to them, He was received into Heaven, and sat down at the right hand of God.

And they went out and preached everywhere, while the Lord worked with them and confirmed the word by the signs that followed.

And they promptly reported all these instructions to Peter and his companions. And after that, Jesus Himself sent out through them, from east to west, the sacred and imperishable proclamation of eternal salvation.

Mark 16:15-20

It is written that Jesus came into Galilee preaching the Gospel of God and saying, "The time is fulfilled, Repent and believe in the Gospel."

Mark 1:14-15

It is written that these are the words of Jesus Christ when He appeared to His disciples after His resurrection, according to John: 'Peace be with you, as the Father has sent Me, I also send you.' And when He said this, He breathed on them, and said to them, **'Receive the Holy Spirit. If you forgive the sins of any, their sins have been forgiven them; if you retain the sins of any, they have been retained.'**

John 20:21, 23

The Gospel of Matthew says this about the great commission: **It is written** that Jesus appeared to the disciples and said; 'All authority has been given to Me in heaven and on earth. Go therefore and make disciples of all the nations, baptizing them in the name of the Father and of the Son and of the Holy Spirit, teaching them to observe all that I commanded you And lo, I am with you always, even to the end of the age.'

Matthew 28:18-20

It is written that Jesus Christ said, **'Scripture cannot be broken.'**
John 10:35

Thank You Lord that blessed is the Church who hears the Word of God and observes it. In the name of Jesus Christ.

Luke 11:28

*When I refer to the **Church** in this section, I am referring to the body of Christ which includes every believing Christian, no matter what denomination, Catholic, Protestant, Jew (still God's chosen people since God's Word is the same yesterday, today and tomorrow), no matter what race. Remember Jesus' words, 'Go and preach the Gospel to all nations.' The Body of Christ includes every person who believes that Jesus Christ is the Son of God, was born of a virgin, conceived by the Holy Spirit, died, and on the third day rose from the dead and ascended into Heaven. Jesus commissioned the Church to love the Lord God with all its heart, to love one's neighbor as oneself, to preach the gospel of repentance and forgiveness* *of sins throughout all nations, to cast out demons in His name and to heal the sick.*

Below we find Paul describing Rome in his day, (not many years before the Fall of Rome and not unlike our country today).

For it is written in Romans 1:18-32

(Unbelief and its consequences)

18 For the wrath of God is revealed from Heaven against all ungodliness and unrighteousness of men, who suppress the truth in unrighteousness,

19 because that which is known about God is evident within them: for God made it evident to them.

20 For since the creation of the world His invisible attributes, His eternal power and divine nature, have been clearly seen, being understood through what has been made, so that they are without excuse.

21 For even though they knew God, they did not honor Him as God, or give thanks, but they became futile in their speculations, and their foolish heart was darkened.

22 Professing to be wise, they became fools,

23 and exchanged the glory of the incorruptible God for an image in the form of corruptible man and the birds and four-footed animals and crawling creatures.

24 Therefore God gave them over in the lusts of their hearts to impurity, that their bodies might be dishonored among them.

25 For they exchanged the truth of God for a lie, and worshiped and served the creature rather than the Creator, who is blessed forever. Amen.

26 For this reason God gave them over to degrading passion: for their women exchanged the natural function for that which is unnatural,

27 and in the same way also the men abandoned the natural function of the woman and burned in their desire toward one an-

other, men with men committing indecent acts and receiving in their own persons the due penalty of their error.

28 And just as they did not see fit to acknowledge God any longer, God gave them over to a depraved mind, to do those things which are not proper,

29 being filled with all unrighteousness, fornication, wickedness, greed, evil, full of envy, murder, strife, deceit, malice, they are gossips,

30 slanderers, haters of God, insolent, arrogant, boastful, inventors of evil, disobedient to parents,

31 without understanding, untrustworthy, unloving, unmerciful;

32 and although they know the ordinance of God, that those who practice such things are worthy of death, they not only do the same, but also give hearty approval to those who practice them.'

Our world today definitely needs to repent, to forgive and to receive the healing touch of Jesus Christ. When the **Church** *is in one accord carrying out Jesus' original commission "to open eyes so that all people may turn from darkness to light, and from the dominion of satan to God, in order that all may receive forgiveness of sins and an inheritance among those who have been sanctified by faith in Jesus Christ" (Acts 26:18 Jesus' words to Paul!)* **then and only then will the church accomplish the true commission of Jesus Christ.**

Then the healing will begin. Remember the words of the Holy Spirit, 'They have eyes to see, but do not see, ears to hear but do not hear; for they are a rebellious house.' (Ezekiel12:2). 'Lest they should see with their eyes, and hear with their ears and understand with their hearts and return, and I should heal them' (Acts 28:27).

Romans 1:18-32 is not meant for judgment, but for describing our chaotic world today, a grim picture to say the least. However, God's unrelenting love from which nothing can separate any of us, and His saving grace are always present to bring forgiveness to the worst of sinners, to bring hope to the lost... to set the captives free... to bring rebirth to the dead in spirit.

Thanks be to God that He can and will accomplish all of this when one repents and is baptized in the name of Jesus Christ for the forgiveness of sins and receives the gift of the Holy Spirit and 'performs deeds appropriate to repentance' (Acts 26:20).

Please pray:

• for repentance for the Church, all nations, all states, all towns, all people! May they all 'repent and believe in the Gospel' Mark 1:15.

• that the love of Christ through His Word will redeem His Church, and His World.

• that the Church will come into the bond of unity, and fervently recommit in one accord to the commission that our Lord Jesus Christ gave to His disciples in the beginning.

• Thank you Lord that the Church will open all eyes so that all may turn from darkness to light, and from the dominion of satan to God, in order that all may receive forgiveness of sins and an inheritance among those who have been sanctified by faith in Jesus Christ.

Acts 26:18

• Thank you Lord that Jesus will sanctify the Church, having cleansed Her by the washing of water with the Word that He will present the Church to Himself as a glorious Church, not having spot or wrinkle, or any such thing; but that the Church should be holy and without blemish. In the name of Jesus Christ.

Ephesians 5:26-27

• Thank You Lord that the Church will be brought to complete unity to let the world know that You sent Jesus and have loved the Church and us even as You have loved Jesus. In the name of Jesus Christ.

John 17:23

Additional Scriptures for Church on pages 58-64

THE LAST SUPPER – HOLY COMMUNION

It is written: And as they were eating, Jesus took bread and broke it, and blessed it and gave it to His disciples and said:

"Take and eat, this is My Body."

Then He took the cup of wine and gave thanks and gave it to them saying:

"Drink from it, all of you, for this is My Blood of the New Covenant, which is shed for many for the remission of sins. Do this in remembrance of Me."

The Last Supper – Holy Communion is the symbol of agreement between God and all people who confess Jesus as the son of the living God. In taking part in the Last Supper - Holy Communion, by eating the bread, the symbol of Christ's Body, and drinking the wine, the symbol of His shed blood, we are confessing belief that Jesus is the Son of God and standing on the faith of His promises that He died for our sins – past, present, and future sins.

It is written: "If we confess our sins, He is faithful to forgive us our sins and cleanse us from all unrighteousness" (Repentance Prayer page 22).

It is also written: "If we forgive the sins of others against us, He will forgive our sins, but if we retain the sins of others against us He will retain our sins" (page 19, The Forgiveness Prayer, Matthew 6:14).

There is such a release of power, Holy Spirit Renewal and healing in the Holy Communion when it is preceded with repentance and forgiveness. Blessings abound as we do all of this in remembrance of Him! Whether you take part in the Lord's supper in Church once a month, once a week, once a day, or take part in a prayer group or as an individual – you are being obedient to our Lord in remembering Him and what He has done for us.

Matthew 26:26-29   Mark 14:22-26   Luke 23: 17-20
I Corinthians 11:23-26

SCRIPTURAL PRAYERS

PRAISE THE LORD

Praise be to His glorious name forever; and may the whole earth be filled with His glory! Amen and Amen!

Psalm 72:19

The Lord lives! Praise be to my Rock. Exalted be God, my Savior!

Psalm 18:46 (NIV)

Thank You Lord, Oh Lord, You are my God; I will exalt You, I will give thanks to Your name; for You have worked wonders, plans formed long ago, with perfect faithfulness! In the name of Jesus Christ.

Isaiah 25:1

Thank You Lord that You are my strength and my song and You have become my salvation! You are my God, and I will extol You! In the name of Jesus Christ.

Exodus 15:2-3

I proclaim the name of the Lord; ascribe greatness to His name! In the name of Jesus Christ.

Deuteronomy 32:3

Thank You Lord that I will bless the Lord who has counselled me; indeed my mind instructs me in the night. I have set the Lord continually before me. Because He is at my right hand, I will not be shaken. In the name of Jesus Christ.

Psalm 16:7-8

Praise the Lord all nations, laud Him, all peoples! For His loving kindness is great towards us, and the truth of the Lord is everlasting. Praise the lord! In the name of Jesus Christ.

Psalm 117

Thank You Lord that our mouths will speak the praise of the Lord, and all flesh will bless His Holy Name forever and ever. In the name of Jesus Christ.

Psalm 145:21

Thank You Lord that we will praise the Lord. Praise Oh servants of the Lord. Let the name of the Lord be praised both now and forever more. From the rising of the sun to the place where it sets the name of the Lord be praised! In the name of Jesus Christ.

Psalm 113:3

Praise the Lord!
Praise the Lord from the heavens;
Praise Him in the heights!
Praise Him, all His angels!
Praise Him, all His hosts!
Praise Him, sun and moon!
Praise Him all stars of light!
In the name of Jesus Christ.
Praise the Lord!

Psalm 148:13

Praise the Lord!
praise God in His sanctuary,
We praise You in Your mighty expanse.
We praise You for Your mighty deeds;
We praise You according to Your excellent greatness.
We praise You with trumpet sound;
We praise You with harp and lyre.
We praise You with timbrel and dancing;
We praise You with stringed instruments and pipe.
We praise You with loud cymbals.

Thank You Lord that everything
that has breath praises the Lord.
Praise the Lord!
In the name of Jesus Christ.

Psalm 150:1-6

More praise - praise Him! Psalms 145-150. Praise Him! Praise Him! Praise Him! Praise Him, for the Lord inhabits the praise of His people. May we be blessed as we praise Him.

SCRIPTURAL PRAYERS FOR THE UNITY AND HEALING OF THE CHURCH

Thank You Lord that the glory which God has given You, You have given to Your Church that they may be one, just as You and God are one; You are in Your Church, and God in You, that Your Church will be perfected in unity, that the world may know that the Father sent You, and loved the Church, even as the Father loved You. In the name of Jesus Christ.

John 17:22-23

Thank You Lord that the Church will open eyes so that all people may turn from darkness to light and from the dominion of satan to God, in order that all may receive forgiveness of sins and an inheritance among those who have been sanctified by faith in You. In the name of Jesus Christ. *(Jesus' commission to Paul)*.

Acts 26:18

Thank You Lord that the Church will repent and be baptized in the Holy Spirit, everyone of them for the remission of sins, and they will receive the gift of the Holy Spirit. In the name of Jesus Christ.

Acts 2:38

Thank You Lord that You might sanctify the Church, having cleansed Her by the washing of water with the Word, that You might present to Yourself the Church in all Her glory, having no spot or wrinkle or any such thing: but that She should be holy and blameless. In the name of Jesus Christ.

Ephesians 5:26-27

Thank You Lord that Your Church may walk in a manner worthy of the God who calls the Church into His own kingdom and glory. And for this reason the Church will constantly thank God that when they receive from the Apostles the Word of God's message, the Church, all bishops, priests, pastors, clergy, laymen, and all parishes will accept it not as the mere word of men, but for what it really is, the Word of God, which also performs its work in all of these people that believe. In the name of Jesus Christ.

1 Thessalonians 2:13

Thank You Lord that You will cleanse Your Church from all defilement of flesh and spirit that we might perfect holiness in fear of the Lord. In the name of Jesus Christ.

II Corinthians 7:1

Thank You Lord that the Church will not break Scripture, for You tell us that Scripture cannot be broken. In the name of Jesus Christ. *(The words of Jesus Christ)*

John 10:35

Thank You Lord that You are the Church's God, and the Church is of Your pasture, and sheep of Your hand. Today, if the Church hears Your voice, it will not harden its heart. In the name of Jesus Christ.

Psalm 95:7

Thank You Lord that the Church will abstain from sexual immorality for it is Your will for the Church's sanctification. In the name of Jesus Christ.

1 Thessalonians 4:3

Thank You Lord that as the angel of God so is the Church, to discern good and evil. And may You, Lord, the Lord our God, be with the Church. In the name of Jesus Christ.

2 Samuel 14:17

Thank You Lord that blessed is the Church who hears the Word of God and observes it. In the name of Jesus Christ.

Luke 11:28

Thank You Lord that all churches, ministers, clergy, priests, bishops, lay ministers, religious leaders and religious counsellors will speak and teach correctly, that they are not partial to any, but teach the way of God in truth. In the name of Jesus Christ.

Luke 20:21

Thank You Lord that the Church will not be ashamed of the gospel, for it is the power of God for salvation to everyone who believes, to the Jew first and also to the Greek (Gentiles). In the name of Jesus Christ.

Romans 1:16

Thank You Lord that every member of Your Church will be born of God, they will overcome the world; and this is the victory that has overcome the world, their faith. And who is the one who overcomes the world but he who believes that Jesus is the Son of God. In the name of Jesus Christ.

1 John 5:4-5

Thank You Lord for purging the Church from all evil. Thank You Lord that Your Glory will fill the Church. In the name of Jesus Christ.

Deuteronomy 19:19, Exodus 40:34

Thank You Lord that the Church will be filled with the knowledge of Your will in all spiritual wisdom and understanding. In the name of Jesus Christ.

Colossians 1:9

Thank You Lord that You Who give perseverance and encouragement grant the Church to be of the same mind with one another according to Christ Jesus; that with one accord the Church may with one voice glorify the God and Father of our Lord Jesus Christ. Wherefore accept one another, just as Christ also accepted them to the glory of God. In the name of Jesus Christ.

Romans 15:5-7

Thank You Lord that Your Church will devote itself to prayer and to the ministry of the Word. In the name of Jesus Christ.

Acts 6:4

Thank You Lord that Your Church will obey God rather than men. In the name of Jesus Christ.

Acts 5:29

Thank You Lord that all denominations be in one accord and <u>proclaim repentance for the forgiveness of sins in Your name to all nations,</u> beginning from Jerusalem. In the name of Jesus Christ. (Commission Jesus gave His disciples!)

Luke 24:47

Thank You Lord that Your Church will discipline itself for the purpose of godliness. In the name of Jesus Christ.

1 Timothy 4:7

Thank You Lord that You will sanctify the Church in the truth. Your Word is truth. In the name of Jesus Christ.

John 17:17

Thank You Lord that You will give all Church leaders utterance and wisdom which none of their opponents will be able to resist or refute. In the name of Jesus Christ.

Luke 21:15

Thank You Lord that whatever was written in earlier times was written for the Church's instruction, that through perseverance and the encouragement of the Scriptures the Church might have hope. In the name of Jesus Christ.

Romans 15:4

Thank You Lord that Your Church, priests, pastors, clergy and lay ministers, practice the truth, come to the light, that their deeds may be manifested as having been wrought in God. In the name of Jesus Christ.

John 2:21

Thank You Lord that the Church will abide in Your Word, then they will truly be disciples of Yours and they will know the truth and the truth will set them free. In the name of Jesus Christ.

John 8:31-32

Thank You Lord that You will open the minds of all Churches, clergy, and all involved in the Church to understand scriptures. In the name of Jesus Christ.

Luke 24:45

Thank You Lord that men in every place will pray. In the name of Jesus Christ.

1 Timothy 2:8

Thank You Lord that the Spirit of truth will guide the Church and all involved in the Church into all truth: for He will not speak on His own initiative but whatever He hears He will speak and He will disclose to the Church what will come. He will glorify You Lord, for He will take of Yours, and disclose it to the Church. All things that the Father has are Yours Lord. Therefore You said that He takes

of Yours, and will disclose it to Your Church. In the name of Jesus
Christ.

John 16:13-15

Thank You Lord that You will make all prophets, evangelists, pastors, teachers, men and women of God of the Churches' joy complete by making them of the same mind, maintaining the same love,
united in Spirit and intent on the same purpose, they will do nothing
from selfishness or empty conceit, but with humility of mind let
each of them regard one another as more important than themselves.
In the name of Jesus Christ.

Philippians 2:2-3

Thank You Lord that You are the Lord of the Church's peace. You
have made the Church one and broken down all the barriers of the
dividing wall. In the name of Jesus Christ.

Ephesians 2:14

Thank You Lord that the Church is putting on the new self who
is being renewed to a true knowledge according to the image of
the One who created the Church – a renewal in which there is no
distinction between Protestant, Catholic, or any denomination, Gen-
tile and Jew, circumcised and uncircumcised, barbarian, slave and
freeman, but Christ is all, and in all. And so as those who have been
chosen of God, holy and beloved, we put on a heart of compassion,
kindness, humility, gentleness, and patience. Bearing with one another, and forgiving each other, whoever has a complaint against
anyone, just as the Lord forgave us, so also should we forgive them
and beyond all these things put on love, which is the perfect bond
of unity. And let the peace of Christ rule in the heart of the Church
to which the Church was called in one body: and be thankful. Let
the Word of Christ richly dwell within the Church with all wisdom,
teaching and admonishing one another with Psalms, and hymns and
spiritual songs, singing with thankfulness in our hearts to God. And
whatever the Church does in word or deed, do all in the name of
the Lord Jesus, giving thanks through Him to God the Father. In the
name of Jesus Christ.

Colossians 3:10-17

Thank You Lord that when trumpeters and the singers make themselves heard with one voice to praise and glorify the Lord, and when they lift up their voice accompanied by trumpets and cymbals and instruments of music, and when they praise the Lord, saying, 'He indeed is good, for His loving kindness is everlasting,' then the house, the house of the Lord, will be filled with a cloud, so that the priests cannot stand to minister because of the cloud, for the glory of the Lord will fill the house of God. In the name of Jesus Christ.

2 Chronicles 5:13-14

Thank You Lord that the Church and all involved with Your Church believe in You and from their innermost beings shall flow rivers of living waters. In the name of Jesus Christ.

John 7:38

Thank You Lord that all churches will become houses of prayer, and the altars of these houses of prayer will be filled with the glory of the Lord! In the name of Jesus Christ. Matthew 21:13, Isaiah 56:7, 2 Chronicles 5:14.

Thank You Lord that the Church will repent and believe in the Gospel. In the name of Jesus Christ. *(The words of Jesus Christ)*

Mark1:1

Thank You Lord that we kneel before You from whom your whole family in heaven and on earth derives its name. We pray that out of Your glorious riches You may strengthen every member of the church and specially our church _____
(name your church) with power through Your Holy Spirit in our inner being, so that Christ may dwell in our hearts through faith. And I pray that all of these people, being rooted and grounded in love, may have power together with all the saints to grasp how wide and long and high and deep is the love of Christ, and to know this love that surpasses all knowledge, that every member of the Church may be filled to the measure of all the fullness of God. We thank You Lord that You who are able to do immeasurably more than all we ask or imagine, according to Your power that is at work within us. To You

be the glory in the Church and in Christ Jesus throughout all generations, forever and ever. Amen in the name of Jesus Christ.

Eph. 3:14-20

Thank You Lord that we will keep Your Sabbath holy between us. Then we will know that You are the Lord our God. In the name of Jesus Christ.

Ezekiel. 20:20

Thank You Lord that the Message of the Lord will spread rapidly and be honored, and thank You Lord that all who serve You will be delivered from wicked and evil men, for not everyone has faith. In the name of Jesus Christ.

II Thessalonians 2:10

PRAYERS FOR THE PEACE OF ISRAEL

The Lord tells us to pray for the peace of Jerusalem. May we honor Him in our obedience to do so!

Thank You Lord for Israel. Theirs is the adoption to sonship; theirs the divine glory, the covenants, the receiving of the law, the temple worship and the promises. Theirs are the patriarchs, and from them is traced the human ancestry of the Messiah, who is God over all, forever praised! Amen.

Romans 9:4-5

Thank You Lord that all Israel will be saved. In the name of Jesus Christ.

Romans 11:26

Thank You Lord that Israel will hope in the Lord for with You there is loving kindness, and with You Lord there is abundant redemption, and You will redeem Israel from all his iniquities. In the name of Jesus Christ.

Psalm 130:7-8

Thank You Lord that Israel will shout aloud! Be glad and rejoice with all Your heart, Oh Daughter of Jerusalem! Thank You Lord that You have taken away Israel's punishment, You have turned back Israel's enemy.

Thank You Lord that You, the King of Israel, are with Israel; never again will Israel fear any harm.

Thank You Lord, that You are with Israel, You are mighty to save. You will take great delight in Israel, You will quiet Israel with Your love, You will rejoice over Israel with singing.

Thank you Lord that you will remove from Israel all who mourn over the loss of their appointed feats - They came from you, O Zion. Thank you that you will remove the burden and reproach.

Thank You Lord that You will rescue the lame and gather those who have been scattered. You Oh Lord will give Israel praise and honor in every land where they have been put to shame. At that time You Oh Lord will gather Israel; at that time You will bring Israel home.

Thank You Lord that You will give honor and praise to Israel among all the peoples of the earth when You restore Israel's fortunes before her very eyes! In the name of Jesus Christ.

Zephaniah 3:14-15, 17-20

Thank You Lord that You will give Israel rest from war. In the name of Jesus Christ.

Joshua 14:15

Thank You Lord that You will give Israel help against the adversary, for deliverance by man is in vain. Through God Israel shall do valiantly; and it is He who will tread down their adversaries. In the name of Jesus Christ.

Psalm 108:13

Thank You Lord that the people who You formed for Yourself, Israel, will declare Your praise. In the name of Jesus Christ.

Isaiah 43:21

Thank You Lord that Israel, the ransomed of the Lord, will return and come with joyful shouting to Zion, with everlasting joy upon their heads. They will find gladness and joy, and sorrow and sighing will flee away. In the name of Jesus Christ.

Isaiah 35:10

Thank You Lord that You will not hide Your face from Israel any longer, for You shall pour out Your spirit on the house of Israel. In the name of Jesus Christ.

Ezekiel 39:29

Thank You Lord that You will cleanse them from all their iniquity by which they have sinned against You, and You will pardon all their iniquities by which they have sinned against You, and by which they have transgressed against You. And they shall be to You a name of joy, a praise and glory before all the nations of the earth, which shall hear of all the good that You do for them, and they shall fear and tremble because of all the good and all the peace that You make for them. In the name of Jesus Christ.

Jeremiah 33:8-9

Thank You Lord that violence will not be heard again in this land, nor devastation or destruction within Israel's borders; but Israel will call her walls salvation, and her gates praise. In the name of Jesus Christ.

Isaiah 60:18

Thank You Lord that You will restore all Israel to the land You gave their forefathers. In the name of Jesus Christ.

Jerimiah 16:18

Thank You Lord that You will bless those who bless Israel and whoever curses Israel. You will curse. In the name of Jesus Christ.

Genesis 12:3

Thank You Lord that You have declared this day Israel as Your people, Your treasured possession as You promised, and that they are to keep all Your commands. Thank You Lord that You have declared that You set Israel in praise, fame and honor high above all the Nations You have made, and that Israel will be a people holy to the Lord God, as You promised. In the name of Jesus Christ.

Dueteronomy 26:18

Thank You Lord that all Israel and all Jews will confess that Jesus is the Son of God, You will abide in them and they in You. In the name of Jesus Christ.

1 John 4:15

Thank You Lord that all Israel and all Jews will repent and each one of them will be baptized in the name of Jesus Christ for the forgiveness of sins and they will receive the gift of the Holy Spirit. In the name of Jesus Christ.

Acts 2:16

Thank You Lord that all Israel and all Jews will be sanctified in the truth: Your Word is truth. In the name of Jesus Christ.

John 17:17

Thank You Lord that all Israel and all Jews will believe in the Lord Jesus Christ and they will be saved, them and their households. In the name of Jesus Christ.

Acts 16:13

OUR NATION – THE WORLD

Thank you for praying for our nation. It seems that violent division, rebellion, immorality and sin are more prevalent today than any other period in the history of our nation. 'Repentance must come or we will all perish.' We must seek the face of God, turn from our wicked ways–repent–forgive and pray.

We as Christians must always remember that judgment, hostility, wrath, evil speaking, evil acts, unforgiveness, and violence are not attributes that lead to peace. Remember that when you are in God's Word you are in the will of God, when you are not, you are running the risk of 'being in the will of satan to do his work'. This does not mean that we are to be weak in our thoughts or deeds. We are to stand firm (on the Word of God), resist the devil, and he will flee. We as prayer warriors must diligently pray for the unity and repentance of our nation, claiming 2 Chronicles 7:14. This will bring healing to our nation.

Before praying the Scriptures for the nation, bind the spirits of division, separation, hatred, violence, anger, rebellion, immorality, denial, idolatry, hostility, hatred of God, defiance, prejudice, unforgiveness, jealousy, greed, evil, and any and all demonic forces that would come against the strength and unity of our nation.

Loose the spirits of love, peace, joy, repentance, forgiveness and unity.

Remember God cannot change a person or situation until we are willing to forgive and repent – not judge. Pray for the hearts of all of us to give up to God, and to forgive! Pray the following Scriptures for repentance and healing of our nation.

The Lord tells us that if a nation does evil in His sight by not obeying His voice, then He will think better of the good with which He had promised to bless it. See Jeremiah 18:10.

O Lord deliver us! Have mercy on us. In the name of Jesus Christ.

Thank You Lord that we Your people which are called by Your Name, shall humble ourselves, and pray, and seek Your face, and turn from our wicked ways: then You will hear from Heaven, and will forgive our sin, and will heal our land. In the name of Jesus Christ.

2 Chronicles 7:14

Thank You Lord that all the world, especially our beloved nation, will keep the charge of the Lord our God, to walk in Your ways, to keep Your statutes, Your commandments, Your ordinances, and Your testimonies, according to what is written in the law of Moses that the world and our nation will succeed in all that we do and wherever we turn. In the name of Jesus Christ.

1 Kings 2:3

Thank You Lord that all inhabitants of our nation and the world will believe in the Lord Jesus Christ, and they will be saved, them and their households. In the name of Jesus Christ.

Acts 16:31

Thank You Lord that all inhabitants of our nation believe that Jesus is the Christ, the Son of God, and that by believing we may have life in His name. In the name of Jesus Christ.

John 20:31

Thank You Lord that all nations of the world put aside all anger, wrath, malice, slander, abusive speech from their mouth. They do not lie to one another, since they have laid aside the old self with their evil practices. In the name of Jesus Christ.

Colossians 3:8-9

Thank You Lord that You will cause all nations to increase and abound in love for one another and for all men, just as they do for You; so that You may establish the hearts of all nations unblameable in holiness before You. In the name of Jesus Christ.

1 Thessalonians 3:12-13

Thank You Lord that You will redeem all nations from their distress. In the name of Jesus Christ.

1 Kings 1:29

Thank You Lord that You will make us a great nation, and You will bless this nation, and make our name great; and so this nation shall be a blessing. In the name of Jesus Christ.

Genesis 12:2

Thank You Lord that all the world, especially this nation, will depart from evil, and do good; We will seek peace and pursue it. In the name of Jesus Christ.

Psalm 34:14

Thank You Lord that all people will come and listen to You, and You will teach us the fear of the Lord. In the name of Jesus Christ.

Psalm 34:11

Thank You Lord that the time is fulfilled; and the Kingdom of God is at hand. Thank You that all nations will repent and believe in the gospel. In the name of Jesus Christ. *(The words of Jesus Christ)*

Mark 1:15

Thank You Lord that You will make known Your salvation; You have revealed Your righteousness in the sight of the nations. In the name of Jesus Christ.

Psalm 98:2

Thank You Lord that You will make us know power and might, and we will know that Your name is the Lord. In the name of Jesus Christ.

Jeremiah 16:21

Thank You Lord that our nation and the world, having the promises of God, will cleanse ourselves from all defilement of flesh and spirit, perfecting holiness in the fear of the Lord. In the name of Jesus Christ.

2 Corinthians 7:1

Thank You Lord that You will fill us with a knowledge of Your will in all spiritual wisdom and understanding, so that this nation and the world may walk in a manner worthy of the Lord, to please You in all respects, bearing fruit in every good work and increasing in the knowledge of God. In the name of Jesus Christ.

Colossians 1:9-10

Thank You Lord that we pray to You that this nation and the world do no wrong, that we will not forget Your teachings, but will let our hearts keep Your commandments. In the name of Jesus Christ.

Proverbs 3:1

Thank You Lord that we will call upon You in the day of trouble. You will rescue our nation and we will honor You. In the name of Jesus Christ.

Psalm 50:15

Thank You Lord that we will cry to God who accomplishes all things for us. He will send from Heaven and save us. You reproach him who tramples on us. You will send forth Your loving kindness and Your truth. In the name of Jesus Christ.

Psalm 57:2-3

Thank You Lord that our nation will abstain from sexual immorality, for it is Your will for our nation, and for our sanctification. In the name of Jesus Christ.

1 Thessalonians 4:3

Thank You Lord that You will wash us thoroughly from any iniquity and cleanse us from our sin. In the name of Jesus Christ.

Psalm 51:2

Thank You Lord that the leaders of this nation, and the world, will put away from themselves a deceitful mouth, and put devious lips far from us. In the name of Jesus Christ.

Proverbs 4:24

Thank You Lord that You have promised, in a favorable time You have answered us, and in a day of salvation You have helped us, and You will keep us and give us a covenant of the people, to restore the land, to make us inherit the desolate heritage: saying to those who are bound, 'Go forth', to those in darkness, 'Show yourselves'. In the name of Jesus Christ.

Isaiah 49:8-9

Thank You Lord that we will obey Your voice and You will be our God, and we will be Your people, and we will walk in the way in which You will command us that it may be well with all of us. In the name of Jesus Christ.

Jeremiah 7:23

Thank You Lord that all people of our nation and the world will submit to You. We will resist the devil, and he will flee from us. We will draw near to God, and God will draw near to us. Cleanse your hands, you sinners, and purify your hearts you double minded. In the name of Jesus Christ.

James 4:7-8

Thank You Lord that You will change Your mind about the harm which You said You will do to Your people. In the name of Jesus Christ.

Exodus 32:14

Thank You Lord that all nations will amend their ways and their deeds, and obey the voice of the Lord their God; and You will change Your mind about the misfortune which You have pronounced against us. In the name of Jesus Christ.

Jeremiah 26:13

Thank You Lord that we pray to You that this nation, our President and the Government, and all world leaders do no wrong, but that they may do what is right, even though they should appear unapproved, for they can do nothing against the truth, only for the truth. In the name of Jesus Christ.

2 Corinthians 13:7-8

Thank You Lord that our nation will not let its faith rest on the wisdom of man, but on the power of God. In the name of Jesus Christ.

I Corinthians 2:5

Thank You Lord that our nation and all of the people who live here will fear the Lord, and hate evil. Pride and arrogance and the evil way, and the perverted mouth, they will hate. In the name of Jesus Christ.

Proverbs 8:13

Thank You Lord that there will be no strange God among us, and thank You that this nation will not worship any foreign Gods. In the name of Jesus Christ.

Psalm 81:9

Thank You Lord that all the earth will fear the Lord; thank You that all the inhabitants of the world stand in awe of You, for You spoke and it was done, You commanded, and it stood fast. Thank You that You nullify the counsel of the nations, You frustrate the plans of the people. In the name of Jesus Christ.

Psalm 33:8-10

Thank You Lord that Your counsel stands forever, the plans of Your heart are from generation to generation, and blessed is our nation whose God is the Lord, the people who You have chosen for Your own inheritance. In the name of Jesus Christ.

Psalm 33:11-12

Thank You Lord that all nations will confess their sins, You are faithful and righteous to forgive us for our sins, and to cleanse us from all unrighteousness. In the name of Jesus Christ.

1 John 1:9

Thank you Lord that You will santify all nations in the truth. Your Word is truth. In the name of Jesus Christ.

John 17:17

Thank You Lord that our leaders will keep their tongues from evil, and their lips from speaking deceit. They will depart from evil and do good. In the name of Jesus Christ.

Psalm 34:13

Thank You Lord that our nation will walk in the way of good men, and keep the path of righteousness. In the name of Jesus Christ.

Proverbs 2:20

Thank You Lord that all nations will enter into a covenant to seek the Lord God with all our hearts and souls. In the name of Jesus Christ.

2 Chronicles 15:12

Thank You Lord that You will rescue the weak and needy of all nations and deliver them out of the hand of the wicked. In the name of Jesus Christ.

Psalm 82:4

Thank You Lord that You protect the strangers, and You support the fatherless and the widows of all nations, but You will thwart the way of the wicked. You will reign forever, Thy God, Oh Zion to all generations. Praise the Lord. In the name of Jesus Christ.

Psalm 146:9-10

Thank You Lord that America and all Nations will see with their eyes, hear with their ears, understand with their hearts, return and You will heal them! In the name of Jesus Christ.

Acts 28:27

Thank You Lord that You will purge the evil from among us. In the name of Jesus Christ.

Deuteronomy 19:19

Thank you Lord that our hearts will be responsive and we will humble ourselves before the Lord when we hear what You have spoken against this place and its people, that we will become accursed and laid waste, and because we will tear our robes and weep in Your presence, You will hear us.

Thank You Lord that behold You will gather all of us, this nation, to our fathers and we will be gathered to our graves in peace, neither will our eyes see all the evil which You will bring to this place. In the name of Jesus Christ.

2 Kings 22:19-20

Thank you Lord that all Americans, and all Nations will tell of Your righteous acts all day long, for those who wanted to harm us have been put to shame and confusion. In the name of Jesus Christ.

Psalm 71:24

Thank you Lord that you will cleanse America and the Nations of the World from all the sin we have committed against You; Thank You Lord that You will forgive all our sins of rebellion against You. Then America and the World will bring You renown joy, praise and honor before all Nations of the World that hear of all the good things that You Oh Lord do for America. And all will be in awe and tremble at the abundant prosperity and peace You provide for Amer- ica. In the name of Jesus Christ.

Jeremiah 33:8-9

Thank You Lord that You will relent from sending calamity to America. In the name of Jesus Christ.

Joel 2:13

Thank You Lord that the name of the Lord is a strong tower and our nation will run to it and be safe. In the name of Jesus Christ.

Proverbs 18:10

Thank You Lord that all families of the Nations will worship You. In the name of Jesus Christ.

Psalm 86:9

Please note thanksgiving for answered prayer page 186.

PRAYERS TO THWART ALL TERRORIST ATTACKS AND GANG-RELATED VIOLENCE

Lord, we thank You that You will thwart every Terrorist plan and gang-related activity which is intended to bring harm to America. Thank You Lord that You will expose all of their activities, their plans, and those people who are behind the plans. We ask that You expose the evil in America. Thank **You,** Lord, for exposing the infiltration of the Muslim Brotherhood into all facets of our Government, even the White House. Thank You Lord for exposing the "Army of Islam," the Black Panthers, and the role they play in the Nation. Thank You for exposing our government's acceptance of these groups and the true intent of these groups. Thank YOU Lord for purging this land from all evil, not only by Your power Lord, but by the people who will rise up to pray for America. **SHINE YOUR LIGHT, LORD, ON ALL THE DARKNESS IN THE US**. Thank You, Lord Jesus, that You will uncover all deception in America. Thank You Lord, that there will be no riots, no civil disobedience or martial law in the coming days, especially around election days. Thank You Lord, that every facet of the media will print and speak truth about all the darkness that has been covered up. You will make all lying lips dumb in all facets of the media and the radio, and if any members of Congress, the Senate, or the House of Representatives or any part of our government, has been involved in any form of bribes or payoffs, that too will be exposed. Lord please, please bless and protect the people who will expose this present darkness in our government in the name of the living Lord Jesus Christ.

I thank You Lord for your protection for all prisoners in America who are being converted to Islam. Thank You Lord, that You will pour out Your Holy Spirit on all of them and they will believe in the Lord Jesus Christ.

Thank You Lord that all people will humble themselves and pray and seek Your face and turn from our wicked ways, and **YOU** Lord will hear from heaven, You will forgive our sins, and You will **HEAL OUR LAND**. Oh God, we thank You, we praise You, we honor You for what You're going to do in America. In the name of **JESUS CHRIST** Lord we thank You that all churches will become **HOUSES OF PRAYER** and men, women, and children everywhere will pray! They will pray thanksgiving for what you have done for America. Lord please deliver us from the addiction of electronic communications and give each one of us a desire to verbally communicate with family and friends and especially with YOU, God. And oh Lord God we praise You for what You're going to do. We plead the blood of Jesus Christ over every single word that I have prayed this day. We ask that Your power, Lord, will be granted to each one of us, Your power and Your Holy Spirit as we listen. And Father God we thank You that we will all, individually and together, go about doing good and healing all who are under the power of Satan, because You God are with us. We praise You, we honor You for being with us during these times. Lord, grant us that extra measure of faith to listen to the words and to pray in the Spirit while listening. We just praise You for that Lord. We praise You and we honor You in the holy name of God. Amen.

You will find an audio version of this prayer at www.theswordofthespiritbook.com under "audio prayers."

ISSUES FOR FASTING AND PRAYER WORLDWIDE

Please Pray scriptures beginning at the bottom of page 79 and page 80 as you lift up the world issues on pages 76-79.

- World leaders – All Political Candidates, all politicians

- The U.S. Government - All Government aides/staffs

- All non-elected government appointed officials and commissions, IRS examiners, Homeland Security, National Security Council, U.S. State Department

- The President, the Vice-President and their families

- The U.S. Cabinet, U.S. Senate, and All Governors

- The U.S. House of Representatives

- The United Nations, all UN and foreign ambassadors

- NATO - National Security Center. All members of NGO's

- All governing bodies throughout entire world. All lobbyists

- All armed forces and their leaders; all war veterans

- U.S. and State Supreme Courts and their judges

- Department of Justice, judges, attorneys, jurors, and their assistants - all legal and clerical assistants

- The police forces, sheriffs, rescue and fire departments

- All State and national law-enforcers - CIA, FBI, DEA, EPA

- The Church - all church denominations, and denominational seminaries, church leaders, bishops, priests, clergy, pastors and their families

- All Christian organizations, all world religious leaders

- The educational system; principals, professors, teachers, lecturers, coaches of universities, colleges, public and private schools, schools for children with special needs

- All students, young people, children, and children in foster care, all parents and families, single parent families; their neighborhoods, all people in homeless missions, and drug rehab centers, veterans hospitals and veterans

- Business leaders, businesses, business employees, all unions, the world economy, US dollar OPEC, fishermen, farmers, agriculturists and food suppliers, all forms of transportation, all energy sources

- The Stock Market – All financial institutions and money managers, Federal Reserve, the SEC, all banks, and all of the employees of all financial institutions. All people making laws and decisions concerning the US economy, IRS

- God's plan for healthcare in America. The medical field for both mental and physical care, specialists, doctors, nurses, technicians, healthcare professionals, home carers, medical researchers, all hospitals, hospice care, all Pharmaceutical companies, FDA

- All scientific research and scientific researchers

- All television and radio stations, broadcasting network programs, talk show hosts and hostesses, all owners, writers, producers, newscasters, crew members, staff, actors, and all advertising sponsors who sponsor any radio or television program, all technicians and all equipment which makes all of the above operable

- All writers, directors, producers of all movies, all schools of cinema and television, students and faculty, and all crew and cameramen responsible for the productions of all movies, Hollywood and the entire entertainment world

- All cinema, television, radio and media personalities, all performing artists, musicians, rock and rap music artists and all of their recordings

- All videos, video games, video programing and programs and all responsible for the production of any video presented to the public. All electronic and solar powered communications

- All computers, world wide web, the internet, internet service providers, cyberspace, computer games, computer programs, computer programers and engineers, and all participants that use or operate computers, computer networks, all bloggers and tweeters, computer highways, all computer data banks, social media participants

- All newspapers, magazines, mailings, all owners, writers, editors, reporters and all media advertising sponsors that sponsor any form of media, all members of the press

- All book publications, authors, editors and book publishers and printing companies, all media advertising agencies

- All toy and game designers and manufacturers

- All sports organizations, sports leagues, sports players, sports fans, sports centers, sports bars, all sport facilities

- The fashion world, all models, all clothes designers, all fashion advertising, fashion magazines

- All special interest groups, all environmentalists and lobbyists, all entitlement groups. These factions, individuals, and groups have a tremendous influence on the public. Let's pray that they will all be in God's will in all that they do. List more of your own.

Thank You Lord that You will protect us and all our families and friends from:

- All chemical, biological and radioactive nuclear attacks, any warfare attacks from outer space, ALL SUICIDE BOMBERS, cyber theft

- All organized crime groups, the sex trade, all sex offenders, sex stalkers, and all kidnappers

- Violent street gangs

- Militant groups, Al-Qaeda, antifa, terrorists and all terrorists cells in America

- Terrorist organizations and activists

- Our prison system, wardens, chaplains, prison guards, prison personnel, prisoners

- Drug lords, drug Cartels, drug pushers, drug manufacturers, drug users, drug growers, all states that have legalized marijuana, all medical marijuana producers and providers

- Writers, directors, producers of horror productions, demonic and satanic horror movies

- All malware specialists in the computer world (i.e. trojans, bugs, time bombs, spam, phishing and pirated software, bloggers and twitters)

- All people involved in identity theft - spyware - viruses, hackers scam artists

- All those responsible for pornography both printed and on the internet, Television, and movies of pornography

- The New Age Movement

- All groups opposing Christian revival and principles in the US Government and our society

- Authorities against Christian principles

- Any and all groups that would choose violence above peace

- All militias against Godly principles who would choose violence above peace

- Politically correct advocates – All anti-American groups and individuals

- All cults and all involved in occult practices

- All secular organizations

- All cultures and religions of the world

- All incurable diseases, viruses, and infections, HPV, H3NZ viruses, Ebola, no flu pandemic in America

- All diseases, coming across the borders

- All new diseases coming into America from foreign nations. May they completely dry up and cause no harm

Please pray scriptures below and on page 80 for people/organizations listed on pages 76-79. If time does not always permit to verbally lift names, just lay hands on the lists and pray scriptures

Thank You Lord that unless they repent, they will all perish. In the name of Jesus Christ. *(The Words of Jesus Christ)*   *Luke 13:5*

Thank You Lord that all the people/groups/organizations that we just lifted to You having the promises of God will cleanse themselves from all defilement of flesh and spirit, perfecting holiness in the fear of the Lord. In the name of Jesus Christ.

2 Corinthians 7:1

Thank You Lord that each one of these people will repent, and each one of them will be baptized in the name of Jesus Christ for the forgiveness of their sins; and they shall receive the gift of the Holy Spirit. For the promise is for them and their children, and for all who are far off, as many as the Lord our God shall call to Himself. May they be saved from this perverse generation. In the name of Jesus Christ.

Acts 2:38

Thank You Lord that all the people we have lifted to You will see with their eyes, hear with their ears, understand with their heart, return and You will heal them. In the name of Jesus Christ.

Acts 28:27

Thank You Lord that all these people and organizations I just lifted to You will confess with their mouths that Jesus is Lord, they will believe in their hearts You God raised Him from the dead, and they will be saved. In the name of Jesus Christ.

Romans 10:9

Thank You Lord that all America will abstain from sexual immoality, for it is Your will for America's sanctification. In the name of Jesus Christ.

1 Thessalonians 4:3

Thank You Lord that You will say to satan, The Lord rebuke you satan! The Lord who has chosen Jerusalem rebuke you in all the lives, situations, and areas we just lifted to the Lord. In the name of Jesus Christ.

Zechariah 3:2

Thousands of intercessors across America are fasting Tuesdays, Wednesdays or Thursdays. Omitting breakfast and lunch as we pray for the issues on pages 76-79. Please join us in this "joint fast" if you are led to do so.

Please see page 172-187 for Praise for answered prayer.

PRAYING FOR YOUR CITY, STATE AND NATION

Please join us in networking across the nation to pray in one accord the powerful Word of God for the healing of our cities and guidance for our local leaders, as well as for the healing of the nation and guidance for our national leaders. Keep it simple by simply praying His Word. Fill in the blanks with the specific name of your town/city. You also may join with other intercessors by setting aside Tuesday or Wednesday for fasting (breakfast and lunch) when praying for these specific needs.

Lift the following names and groups to the Lord and pray the Scriptural Prayers that follow:

- Everyone in our community
- The School Board, all Schools, Principals, Teachers, Students and their Parents, School Personnel, School Food Services, and School Bus Drivers
- Fire and Rescue Departments
- The Police Department, Highway Patrol
- All Prisons, Prisoners, Prison Workers
- All Military Personnel and Military Facilities
- All city transportation systems
- All Judges, Attorneys, Jurors
- City Port Authorities
- All Business Owners, all Businesses, all business employees
- All forms of the Media
- All Utilities Departments
- Tax Appraisers and Tax Collectors
- City Zoning Authorities, City Commissioners
- All Members of City and County Government
- Supervisors of Elections
- All members of City Government
- The Mayor's office, Mayor _____
- All City Council Members (list first names in your city)
- All Churches, Pastors, Church Leaders
- All Medical Facilities, Doctors and Nurses, Drug and Alcohol rehab centers, and homeless missions

- The Governor of _____ All State Legislators & Staff

- President _____, Vice President _____, The Cabinet

- The Supreme Court and Staff

- The Congress, All Whitehouse Staff & National Military

Thank You Lord that our city _____, our state and nation, having the promises of God, will cleanse ourselves from all defilement of flesh and spirit, perfecting holiness in the fear of the Lord. In the name of Jesus Christ.

2 Corinthians 7:1

Thank You Lord that every person and group listed above will be filled with the knowledge of Your Will in all spiritual wisdom and understanding. Thank You Lord that we will repent, and each one will be baptized in the name of Jesus Christ for the forgiveness of our sins. In the name of Jesus Christ.

Col. 1:9, Acts 2:38

Thank You Lord that our city _____, our state and nation will enter into a covenant to seek the Lord God with all our hearts and souls. In the name of Jesus Christ.

2 Chronicles 15:12

Thank You Lord that every member of the _____ City Council, Mayor's office, the leaders and legislators, judges, attorneys, solicitors and jurors will seek to please God, not man. Thank You Lord that we will all fear the Lord and hate evil. In the name of Jesus Christ.

Acts 5:29, Proverbs 8:13

Thank You Lord for purging all leaders, all citizens, all schools and all neighborhoods in our city _____, our state and the nation from all evil. In the name of Jesus Christ.

Deuteronomy 19:19

Thank You Lord that no weapon formed against the city of _____, the state of _____, and our nation will ever prosper and we will refuse every tongue that accuses us. Thank

You that this is the heritage of the servants of the Lord and this is their vindication from You Oh Lord because You have declared it. In the name of Jesus Christ.

Isaiah 54:17

Thank You Lord that You will give all citizens of _____ and our nation an undivided heart and put a new spirit in us. You will remove from us our hearts of stone, and give us hearts of flesh, so we will follow Your decrees, and be careful to keep Your laws. We will be Your people and You will be our God. In the name of Jesus Christ.

Ezekiel 11:19-20

Thank You Lord that there will be no other gods among us in our city _____, our state or nation. Thank You Lord that the city of _____, our state of _____ and our nation will not worship any foreign gods. In the name of Jesus Christ.

Psalm 81:9

Thank You Lord that all the citizens of _____ will confess Jesus before men, and the Son of Man will confess all citizens of _____ before the angels of God. In the name of Jesus Christ. Thank You Lord that no evil will befall our city, state or nation, nor will any plague come near our tent. Thank You Lord that You will protect us from all evil; You will keep our soul. In the name of Jesus Christ.

Luke 12:8, Psalm 91:10, Psalm 121:7-8

Thank You Lord that for six days, work is to be done in the city of _____, the state of _____ and our Nation, but the Sabbath will be a day of rest, Holy to the Lord. In the name of Jesus Christ.

Exodus 31:15

Thank You Lord that our city of _____, our state of _____ and the Nation will remember the Sabbath to keep it holy. In the name of Jesus Christ

Exodus 20:8

Thank You Lord that we will never stop teaching and proclaiming the good news that Jesus is the Christ. Thank You Lord that we will forsake all and follow You. In the name of Jesus Christ.

Acts 5:12

List Your Local Schools _____

_____

_____

_____

Thank You Lord that You will open the eyes of all the students and teachers of the above schools so that they may turn from darkness to light and from the dominion of satan to God, in order that they might receive forgiveness of sins and an inheritance among those who have been sanctified by faith in Jesus Christ. In the name of Jesus Christ.

Acts 26:18

Thank You Lord that these students and teachers will walk in the ways of good men, and keep the paths of the righteous. In the name of Jesus Christ.

Proverbs 2:20

Thank You Lord that all students and teachers of the above schools will abstain from sexual immorality, for it is Your will for them for their sanctification. In the name of Jesus Christ.

1 Thessalonians 4:3

The Lord rebuke you, satan! Indeed, the Lord who chose Jerusalem rebuke you in all the lives of the citizens of _____ and in all situations in our beloved state of _____, and in the nation! In the name of Jesus Christ.

Zechariah 3:2

Please close with the Deliverance Prayer on page 25 and the Liberty Savard Prayer on pages 29-30 of *The Sword of the Spirit The Word of God*.

Lamb's Books, Inc. gives permission to anyone to copy and enlarge pages 75-83 only. Please pass these sheets out to others. Blessings to you!

ADD YOUR OWN ISSUES FOR FASTING AND PRAYER FOR THE WORLD, OUR NATION, YOUR STATE AND CITY

TELLING PEOPLE ABOUT JESUS

Thank You Lord that utterance will be given to us that we may open our mouths boldly to make known the mystery of the Gospel. In the name of Jesus Christ.

Ephesians 6:19

Thank You Lord that You will open a door for our message so that we may proclaim the mysteries of Christ for which we are in chains. We pray that we may proclaim it clearly as we should. In the name of Jesus Christ.

Colossians 4:3-4 (NIV)

Thank You Lord that You will stretch out Your hand, and touch our mouths, and say to us, behold I have put My Words in Your mouth. In the name of Jesus Christ

Jeremiah 1:9

Thank You Lord that the opening of our mouth shall produce right things. For our mouths will utter truth, and wickedness is an abomination to our lips. In the name of Jesus Christ.

Proverbs 8:6-7

Thank You Lord that we will speak boldly with reliance upon the Lord Who will bear witness to the Word of His grace, granting that signs and wonders be done by our hands. In the name of Jesus Christ.

Acts 14:3

Thank You Lord that our message is not in persuasive words of wisdom, but a demonstration of the Spirit and the power; that everyone's faith should not stand on the wisdom of man, but on the power of God. In the name of Jesus Christ.

1 Corinthians 2:4-5

Thank You Lord that we will speak Your testimonies before kings, and shall not be ashamed. We shall delight in Your commandments which we love. In the name of Jesus Christ.

Psalm 119:46-47

Thank You Lord that we cannot be shaken, so let us show gratitude by which we may offer to God an acceptable service with reverence and awe, for our God is a consuming fire. In the name of Jesus Christ.

Hebrews 12:28-29

Thank You Lord that You will bless us with insight and we will shine brightly like the brightness of the expanse of heaven and we will lead many to righteousness like the stars for ever and ever. In the name of Jesus Christ.

Daniel 12:3

Thank You Lord that we will follow You, and become fishers of men. In the name of Jesus Christ.

Mark 1:17

Thank You Lord for putting a message in our mouths. In the name of Jesus Christ.

Numbers 23:5

Thank You Lord that I have not hidden Your righteousness within my heart; I have spoken of Your faithfulness and Your salvation; I have not concealed Your loving kindness and Your truth from the great congregation. In the name of Jesus Christ.

Psalm 40:10

Thank You Lord that You will speak for Your servant is listening. In the name of Jesus Christ.

1 Samuel 3:10

Thank You Lord that we will forsake all and follow You. In the name of Jesus Christ. *Luke 5:11*

Thank You Lord that we will never stop teaching and preaching that Jesus is the Christ. In the name of Jesus Christ.

Acts 5:42

Thank You Lord that we will speak so effectively that a great number of Jews and Gentiles will believe in the name of Jesus. In the name of Jesus Christ.

Acts 14:1

SALVATION

Thank You Lord that they confess with their mouths that Jesus Christ is Lord, and believe in their hearts that You raised Him from the dead, and they will be saved. For with the heart this person believes, resulting in righteousness, and with the mouth he confesses, resulting in salvation. In the name of Jesus Christ.

Romans 10:9-10

Thank You Father that the glory You have given to Jesus, You have given to these people, that they may be one with You just as You and Jesus are one. Jesus is in them, and You are in Jesus in order that they may be perfected in unity, that the world may know that You did send Jesus, and do love them, even as You love Jesus. In the name of Jesus Christ.

John 17:21-23

Thank You Lord that they will confess that Jesus is the Son of God, God will abide in them, and they in God. In the name of Jesus Christ.

1 John 4:15

Thank You Lord that each one of these people will repent, and each one of them will be baptized in the name of Jesus Christ for the forgiveness of their sins; and they shall receive the gift of the Holy Spirit. In the name of Jesus Christ.

Acts 2:38

Thank You Lord that all the people we have lifted to You are filled with joy because they have come to believe in You, them and their whole family. In the name of Jesus Christ.

Acts 16:34

Thank You Lord that You are the way and the truth and the life; no one comes to the Father, but through You Jesus. Thank You Lord, that these people will come to You Father, through Jesus. In the name of Jesus Christ.

John 14:6

Thank You Lord that they will call on Your Name and You will answer them, and You will say, 'They are My people', and they will say, 'The Lord is My God.' In the name of Jesus Christ.

Zechariah 13:9

Thank You Lord that You will be found by those who seek You not, You will become manifest to those who do not ask for You. In the name of Jesus Christ.

Romans 10:20

Thank You Lord that they, having been freed from sin, will become slaves to righteousness. In the name of Jesus Christ.

Romans 6:18

Thank You Lord that You say to those who confess Jesus before men, the Son of Man shall confess them also before the angels of God. In the name of Jesus Christ.

Luke 12:8

Thank You Lord that You have delivered them from the domain of darkness and transferred them to the heavenly Kingdom of Your beloved Son, in whom we have redemption and forgiveness of sins. In the name of Jesus Christ.

Colossians 1:13-14

Thank You Lord that whenever they turn to the Lord, the veil will be taken away. In the name of Jesus Christ.

2 Corinthians 3:16

Thank You Lord that they may know the love of Christ which surpasses knowledge, that they may be filled up to all the fullness of God. In the name of Jesus Christ.

Ephesians 3:19

Thank You Lord that in Christ they are a new creation; the old things have passed away; behold new things have come. In the name of Jesus Christ.

2 Corinthians 5:17

Thank You Lord that You might gather together into one the children of God who are scattered abroad. In the name of Jesus Christ.

John 11:52

Thank You Lord that the time is fulfilled and the Kingdom of God is at hand; thank You Lord that these people will repent and believe in the Gospel. In the name of Jesus Christ.

Mark 1:15

Thank You Lord that You saved them, not on the basis of deeds which they have done in righteousness, but according to Your mercy, by the washing of regeneration and renewing by the Holy Spirit. Whom You poured out upon them richly through Jesus Christ our Savior. In the name of Jesus Christ.

Titus 3:5-6

Thank You Lord that the one who overcomes the world, is the one who believes that Jesus is the Son of God. In the name of Jesus Christ.

1 John 5:5

Thank You Lord that You have chosen them from the beginning for salvation through sanctification by the Spirit and faith in the truth. In the name of Jesus Christ.

2 Thessalonians 2:13

Thank You Lord that the Son of Man has come to seek and to save those who were lost. In the name of Jesus Christ.

Luke 19:10

Thank You Lord that now in Christ Jesus those who formerly were far off have been brought near by the blood of Christ. In the name of Jesus Christ.

Ephesians 2:13

Thank You Lord that You desire these people to be saved and to come to the knowledge of the truth. In the name of Jesus Christ.

1 Timothy 2:3-4

Thank You Lord that the eyes of their hearts may be enlightened, so that they may know what is the hope of Your calling, what are the riches of the glory of Your inheritance in the saints and what is the surpassing greatness of Your power toward those who believe. In the name of Jesus Christ.

Ephesians 1:18

Thank You Lord that You say; 'At the acceptable time I listened to you, and on the day of salvation I helped you.' Behold, now is the 'acceptable time', behold, now is the 'day of salvation'. In the name of Jesus Christ.

2 Corinthians 6:2

Thank You Lord that they believe that Jesus is the Christ, the Son of God, and that by believing they may have life in His name. In the name of Jesus Christ.

John 20:31

Thank You Lord that You are the light of the world. Whoever follows You will never walk in darkness, but have the light of life. Thank You Lord that these people will follow You. In the name of Jesus Christ.

John 8:12

Thank You Lord that these people have not received a spirit of slavery leading to fear again but they have received a spirit of adoption as sons by which they cry out 'Abba Father.' The Spirit bears witness with their spirit that they are children of God. In the name of Jesus Christ.

Galatians 4:6

Thank You Lord that You have given them/us eternal life, and this life is in Your Son. Thank You that those who have the Son have the life; those who do not have the Son of God do not have the life. In the name of Jesus Christ.

1 John 5:11-12

Thank You Lord that they will believe that Jesus Christ is the Son of God. In the name of Jesus Christ.

Acts 8:37

Thank You Lord that even when they were dead in their transgressions, You made them alive together with Christ (by grace they have been saved). In the name of Jesus Christ.

Ephesians 2:5

Thank You Lord that we will put aside the deeds of darkness and put on the armor of light. In the name of Jesus Christ.

Romans 13:12

Thank You Lord that Your hand is with them and these people will believe and turn to the Lord. In the name of Jesus Christ.

Acts 11:21

Thank You Lord that they will turn to God and repent and have faith in the Lord Jesus Christ. In the name of Jesus Christ.

Acts 20:21

Thank You Lord that through Your name everyone who believes in You receives forgiveness of sins. In the name of Jesus Christ.

Acts 10:43

Thank You Lord that You will demonstrate Your perfect patience, as an example for those who would believe in You for eternal life. In the name of Jesus Christ.

1 Timothy 1:16

Thank You Lord that You are faithful, and have called us into fellowship with Your Son, Jesus Christ our Lord. In the name of Jesus Christ.

1 Corinthians 1:9

Thank You Lord that at the name of Jesus every knee will bow, those who are in heaven, and on earth, and under the earth, and every tongue will confess that Jesus Christ is Lord, to the glory of God the Father. In the name of Jesus Christ.

Philippians 2:10-11

FOR THE LOST — THE BACKSLIDER

Thank You Lord that these people will repent, and turn away from all of their transgressions, so that iniquity may not become a stumbling block for them. In the name of Jesus Christ.

Ezekiel 18:30

Thank You Lord that though they were going astray like sheep, but now they have returned to their shepherd and guardian of their souls. In the name of Jesus Christ.

1 Peter 2:25

Thank You Lord that You have wiped out their transgressions like a thick cloud, and their sins like a heavy mist; they will return to You, for You have redeemed them. In the name of Jesus Christ.

Isaiah 44:22

Thank You Lord that You take no pleasure in the death of the wicked, but rather that the wicked turn back from their evil ways. Thank You that they will turn back from their evil ways. In the name of Jesus Christ.

Ezekiel 33:11

Thank You Lord that they will say 'Come let us return to the Lord, for He has torn us, but He will heal us, He has wounded us, but He will bandage us. He will revive us after two days, He will raise us up on the third day, that we may live before Him. So let us press on to know the Lord. His going forth is as certain as the dawn; and He will come to us like the rain, like the spring rain watering the earth.' In the name of Jesus Christ.

Hosea 6:1-3

Thank You Lord that these people will return, You will heal their faithlessness, behold they come to You, for You are the Lord their God. In the name of Jesus Christ.

Jeremiah 3:22

Thank you Lord that You will frown on them no longer for You are merciful. You will not be angry forever if they only acknowledge their guilt - they have rebelled against the Lord their God. You will cure them of backsliding. In the name of Jesus Christ.

Jeremiah 3:12-13, 22

TO RECEIVE THE BAPTISM OF
THE HOLY SPIRIT

Thank You Lord that each one of these people-will repent and be baptized in the name of Jesus Christ for the forgiveness of sins; and they shall receive the gift of the Holy Spirit. For the promise is for them and their children, and for all who are far off, as many as the Lord our God will call unto Himself. They will be saved from this perverse generation. In the name of Jesus Christ.

Acts 2:38-39

Thank You Lord that the eyes of their/our heart will be enlightened, so that they/we may know what is the hope of Your calling, what are the riches of the glory of Your inheritance in the saints. In the name of Jesus Christ.

Ephesians 1:18

Thank You Lord that the Spirit of Him who raised Jesus Christ from the dead dwells in them. You who raised Jesus Christ from the dead will also give life to their mortal bodies through Your Spirit who indwells in them, so then these people are under obligation not to the flesh to live according to the flesh, for if they are living according to the flesh, they must die, but if by the Spirit they are putting to death the deeds of the body, they will live. For all of them are being led by the Spirit of God, they are sons of God. In the name of Jesus Christ.

Romans 8:11-14

Thank You Lord that this is Your commandment that they believe in the name of Your Son, Jesus Christ, and love one another, just as You commanded them. And those who keep Your commandments abide in You and You in them. And we know by this that You abide in them by the Spirit whom You have given them. In the name of Jesus Christ.

1 John 3:23-24

Thank You Lord that You will baptize them with the Holy Spirit and fire. In the name of Jesus Christ.

Luke 3:16

Thank You Lord that they are a temple of God, and that the Spirit of God dwells in them. In the name of Jesus Christ.

1 Corinthians 3:16

Thank You Lord that they would ask You, and You would give them living water. In the name of Jesus Christ.

John 4:10

Thank You Lord that You have promised that they are the temple of the living God, that You dwell in them, and walk among them and You will be their God, and they shall be Your people. In the name of Jesus Christ.

2 Corinthians 6:16

Blessed be the God and Father of Our Lord Jesus Christ who according to His great mercy has caused all of these people to be born again to a living hope through the resurrection of Jesus Christ from the dead. In the name of Jesus Christ.

1 Peter 1:3

Thank You Lord that You will direct their hearts into the love of God, and into the steadfastness of Christ. In the name of Jesus Christ.

2 Thessalonians 3:5

Thank You Lord that You, Who commanded the light to shine out of darkness, are the One Who has shone in their hearts to give the light of the knowledge of Your Glory in the face of Jesus. In the name of Jesus Christ.

2 Corinthians 4:6

Thank You Lord that all these people will turn to Your reproof, and You will pour out Your Spirit on them and make Your Word known to them. In the name of Jesus Christ.

Proverbs 1:23

Thank You Lord that they will all be filled with the Holy Spirit and begin to speak with other tongues, as the Spirit gives them utterance. In the name of Jesus Christ.

Acts 2:4

Thank You Lord that You are sending forth the promise of God upon them, and they will be clothed with power from on high. In the name of Jesus Christ.

Luke 24:49

Thank You Lord that they will be baptized with the Holy Spirit not many days from now. In the name of Jesus Christ.

Acts 1:5

Thank You Lord that You would grant all of them according to the riches of Your glory to be strengthened with power through Your Holy Spirit in their inner man, so that Christ may dwell in their hearts through faith, and that they being rooted and grounded in love, may be able to comprehend with all the saints what is the breadth, length, height and depth and to know the love of Christ, which surpasses knowledge, that they may be filled up to all the fullness of God. In the name of Jesus Christ.

Ephesians 3:16-19

Thank You Lord that as many as received You, to them You give the right to become children of God, even to those who believe in Your name, who were born not of blood, nor the will of the flesh, nor the will of man, but of God. In the name of Jesus Christ.

John 1:12-13

Thank You Lord that You will pour out Your love into their hearts by the Holy Spirit whom You have given them. In the name of Jesus Christ.

Romans 5:5

Thank You Lord that these people have received the Holy Spirit just as we did. In the name of Jesus Christ.

Acts 10:47

Thank you Lord that the Spirit of the Lord will come upon them mightily, they shall prophesy and be changed into another man. In the name of Jesus Christ.

1 Samuel 10:6

Thank You Lord that all these people keep Your commandments, and Your commandments are not burdensome. In the name of Jesus Christ.

1 John 5:3

Thank You Lord that these people will be born of God, they will overcome the world: and this is the victory that has overcome the world – their faith. In the name of Jesus Christ.

1 John 5:4

Thank You Father, that You, who know the hearts of these people, bear witness to them, giving them the Holy Spirit, just as You also have done to us. In the name of Jesus Christ.

Acts 15:8

Thank You Lord that You said, 'they who believe in Jesus, as the scripture says, from their innermost being shall flow rivers of living water.' In the name of Jesus Christ.

John 7:38

Thank You Lord that these people have received not the spirit of the world, but the Spirit who is from God that they may know the things freely given to them by God. In the name of Jesus Christ.

1 Corinthians 2:12

Thank You Lord that You will anoint us with the Holy Spirit and with power, and we will go about doing good, and healing all who are oppressed by the devil; for You are with us. In the name of Jesus Christ.

Acts 10:38

Thank You Lord that You give the Spirit without limit. In the name of Jesus Christ.

John 3:31

Thank You Lord that we are all filled with joy and the Holy Spirit. In the name of Jesus Christ.

Acts 13:52

Thank You Lord that according to Your great mercy You have caused us to be born again to a living hope through the resurrection of Jesus Christ from the dead, to obtain an inheritance which is imperishable and undefiled and will not fade away, reserved in heaven for us, who are protected by the power of God through faith for a salvation ready to be revealed in the last time. In the name of Jesus Christ.

1 Peter 1:3-5

Thank You Lord for how much more shall their heavenly Father give the Holy Spirit to those who ask. In the name of Jesus Christ.

Luke 11:13

Thank You Lord that the gift of the Holy Spirit will be poured out on all the people we have lifted to you (especially our family members) and they will be heard speaking in tongues and praising God. In the name of Jesus Christ.

Acts 10:44

Thank You Lord that You give the Holy Spirit to those who obey You. In the name of Jesus Christ.

Acts 5:32

Thank You Lord that we will do everything You say, we will obey You. In the name of Jesus Christ.

Exodus 24:7

Thank You Lord that these people will ask. In the name of Jesus Christ.

INNER HEALING

For those whose lives are affected as a result of childhood traumas, abuse or past hurts, those with depression, addictive behavior, oppression and mental illness. These Scriptures are often prayed in conjunction with the Deliverance Scriptures since symptoms or problems are similar and often overlap.

Thank You Lord that You will search them/us Oh God, and know their/our heart, try them/us and know their/our anxious thoughts, and see if there be any hurtful way in them/us, and lead them/us in the everlasting way. In the name of Jesus Christ.

Psalm 139:23-24

Thank You Lord that You will turn to them and be gracious to them, for they are lonely and afflicted. The troubles of their heart are enlarged; bring them out of their distresses. Look upon their affliction and their trouble and forgive all of their sins. In the name of Jesus Christ.

Psalm 25:16-18

Thank You Lord that they will not be conformed to this world, but they are transformed by the renewing of their mind, that they may prove what the will of God is, that which is good and acceptable and perfect. In the name of Jesus Christ.

Romans 12:2

Thank You Lord that You will bring their soul out of prison, so that they may give thanks to Your name. The righteous will surround them, and You Lord will deal bountifully with them. In the name of Jesus Christ.

Psalm 142:7

Thank You Lord that they will speak the truth in love, and they will grow up in all aspects into Him who is the head, even Christ. In the name of Jesus Christ.

Ephesians 4:15

> *This verse is helpful in finding the root cause of the person's problem.*
>
> **Thank You Lord that all things become visible when exposed by the light, for everything that becomes visible is light, for this reason it says awake sleeper and rise from the dead, and Christ will shine on them. In the name of Jesus Christ.**
>
> *Ephesians 5:13-14*
>
> *Forgiveness is the key to much healing!*
>
> **Thank You Lord that they will forgive men their transgressions, so that their heavenly Father will forgive them. In the name of Jesus Christ.**
>
> *Matthew 6:14-15*

Thank You Lord that You are their lamp; You illuminate their darkness. In the name of Jesus Christ.

2 Samuel 22:29

Thank You Lord that You will again have compassion on them. You will tread their iniquities under foot. Yes, You will cast all of their sins into the depths of the sea. In the name of Jesus Christ.

Micah 7:19

Thank You Lord that all of these people will confess their sins, You are faithful and righteous to forgive them their sins, and to cleanse them from all unrighteousness. In the name of Jesus Christ.

1 John 1:9

Thank You Lord that You will accomplish what concerns them. In the name of Jesus Christ.

Psalm 138:8

Thank You Lord that if today they hear Your voice, they will not harden their hearts. In the name of Jesus Christ.

Hebrews 4:7

Thank You Lord that You will acquit them of hidden faults. In the name of Jesus Christ.

Psalm 19:12

Thank You Lord that those who have been troubled with unclean spirits are being cured. In the name of Jesus Christ.

Luke 6:18

Thank You Lord that they will be filled with the knowledge of Your will in all spiritual wisdom and understanding. In the name of Jesus Christ.

Colossians 1:9

Thank You Lord that You did not give them a spirit of fear or timidity, but of power and love and discipline. In the name of Jesus Christ.

2 Timothy 1:7

Thank You Lord that You desire truth in the innermost being, and in the hidden part You will make us know wisdom. In the name of Jesus Christ.

Psalm 51:6

Thank You Lord that You will set our iniquities before You, our secret sins in the light of Your presence. In the name of Jesus Christ.
Psalm 90:8

Thank You Lord that they who have suffered in the flesh have ceased from sin, so as to live the rest of the time in the flesh, no longer for the lusts of men, but for the will of God. In the name of Jesus Christ.

1 Peter 4:1-2

Thank You Lord that they will speak with their mouths what fills their hearts. In the name of Jesus Christ.

Matthew 12:34

Thank You Lord that they joyfully concur with the law of God in their inner man. In the name of Jesus Christ.

Romans 7:22

Thank You Lord that a sword will pierce even their own soul to the end that thoughts from their hearts may be revealed. In the name of Jesus Christ.

Luke 2:35

Thank You Lord that You will create in them a clean heart, and renew a steadfast spirit within them. In the name of Jesus Christ.

Psalm 51:10

Thank You Lord that You will give them one heart, and You will put a new Spirit within them. And You will take the heart of stone out of their flesh and give them a heart of flesh, that they may walk in Your statues and keep Your ordinances and do them. Then they will be Your people and You will be their God. In the name of Jesus Christ.

Ezekiel 11:19

Thank You Lord that they arise, shine, for their light has come and Your Glory has risen upon them. In the name of Jesus Christ.

Isaiah 60:1

Thank You Lord that they will repent therefore and return that their sin may be forgiven (wiped away) in order that times of refreshing may come from the presence of the Lord. In the name of Jesus Christ.

Acts 3:19

Thank You Lord that You will give us life. In the name of Jesus Christ.

1 John 5:16

Thank You Lord that they will seek You, Lord, and You will answer them, and deliver them from all their fears. In the name of Jesus Christ.

Psalm 34:4

Thank You Lord that we will cry to You in our distress, and You will hear and deliver us. In the name of Jesus Christ.

2 Chronicles 20:9

Thank You Lord that You even You are He that blots out our transgressions for Your own sake and remembers our sin no more. In the name of Jesus Christ.

Isaiah 43:25

Thank You Lord that You will circumcise their hearts, and the hearts of their descendants to love the Lord their God with all of their heart and with all of their soul, in order that they may live. In the name of Jesus Christ.

Deuteronomy 30:6

Thank You Lord that nothing in them is hidden that shall not become evident, nor anything secret that shall not be known, and come to light. In the name of Jesus Christ.

Luke 8:17

Thank You Lord that they will describe what great things God has done for them, proclaiming throughout the city what great things Jesus has done for them. In the name of Jesus Christ.

Luke 8:39

Thank You Lord that they were dead and have begun to live, and were lost and have been found. In the name of Jesus Christ.

Luke 15:32

Thank You Lord that You will unbind them, and let them go. In the name of Jesus Christ.

John 11:44

Thank You Lord that the secrets of their hearts will be disclosed, and so they will fall on their faces and worship God, declaring that God is certainly among them. In the name of Jesus Christ.

1 Corinthians 14:25

Thank You Lord that there is nothing covered up in them that will not be revealed, or hidden that will not be known. In the name of Jesus Christ.

Luke 12:2

Thank You Lord that You would grant to them according to Your riches in glory to be strengthened by might by Your Holy Spirit in their inner man, so that Christ may dwell in their hearts through faith, and that they will be rooted and grounded in love, and that they may be able to comprehend with all the saints what is the breadth and length and height and depth, and to know the love of Christ which surpasses knowledge, that they may be filled up to all the fullness of God. In the name of Jesus Christ.

Ephesians 3:16-19

Thank You Lord that blessed are they whose transgressions are forgiven, whose sin is covered, how blessed are they to whom the Lord does not impute iniquity, and in whose spirit there is no deceit. In the name of Jesus Christ.

Psalm 32:1

Thank You Lord that You will restore us, and cause Your face to shine upon us, and we will be saved. In the name of Jesus Christ.

Psalm 80:3

Thank You Lord that though their outer man is decaying, yet their inner man is being renewed day by day. In the name of Jesus Christ.

2 Corinthians 4:16

Thank You Lord that You have seen their ways, but You will heal them, and restore comfort to them, and to their mourners. In the name of Jesus Christ.

Isaiah 57:18

Thank You Lord that with authority and power, You command the unclean spirits and they come out. In the name of Jesus Christ.

Luke 4:36

Thank You Lord that You tell us that greater things we would do than what You did because You are with the Father, and whatever we ask in Your name that will You do, that the Father might be glorified in the Son. In the name of Jesus Christ.

John 12:14

Thank You Lord that You will bring all works into judgment including every secret thing, whether good or evil. In the name of Jesus Christ.

Ecclesiastes 12:14

Remember many of the Deliverance Scriptures (p. 113) can be applied to inner healing.

PHYSICAL HEALING

Thank You Lord that You have promised to pardon all their/our iniquities and to heal all their/our diseases. In the name of Jesus Christ.

Psalm 103:3

Thank You Lord that these people will have the knowledge of salvation by the forgiveness of their sins because of the tender mercy of our God, with which the Sunrise from on high shall visit them, to shine upon those in darkness and the shadow of death, to guide their feet into the way of peace. In the name of Jesus Christ.

Luke 1:77-79

Thank You Lord that You will set free those who are doomed to death. In the name of Jesus Christ.

Psalm 102:20

Thank You Lord that they will not be conformed to this world, but they are transformed by the renewing of their mind, that they may prove what the will of God is, that which is good and acceptable and perfect. In the name of Jesus Christ.

Romans 12:2

Thank You Lord that You will again have compassion on them. You will tread their iniquities under foot. Yes, You will cast all of their sins into the depth of the sea. In the name of Jesus Christ.

Micah 7:19

Thank You Lord that they will not be afraid any longer, they will believe and they shall be made well. In the name of Jesus Christ.

Luke 8:50

Thank You Lord that their sins have been forgiven. Their faith has saved them, they will go in peace. In the name of Jesus Christ.

Luke 7: 48-50

Thank You Lord that they acknowledge their sin to You, and their iniquity they did not hide; they will say, 'I will confess my transgressions to the Lord; and the Lord will forgive the guilt of my sin.' In the name of Jesus Christ.

Psalm 32:5

Thank You Lord that You will heal those who are sick and say to them, 'the Kingdom of God has come near to you.' In the name of Jesus Christ.

Luke 10:9

Thank You Lord that at this very time You will cure these people of diseases and afflictions and evil spirits and You will grant sight to these who are blind. In the name of Jesus Christ.

Luke 7:21

Thank You Lord that this sickness is not unto death, but for the glory of God that the Son of God might be glorified by it. In the name of Jesus Christ.

John 11:4

Thank You Lord that You will bring them health and You will cure them, and reveal unto them an abundance of peace and truth. In the name of Jesus Christ.

Jeremiah 33:6

Thank You Lord that the eyes of those who see will not be blinded, and the ears of those who hear will listen. In the name of Jesus Christ.

Isaiah 32:3

Heal them Oh Lord, and they will be healed, save them and they will be saved. In the name of Jesus Christ.

Jeremiah 17:14

Thank You Lord that they will confess their sins to one another and pray for one another so that they may be healed. The effective prayer of a righteous man can accomplish much. In the name of Jesus Christ.

James 5:16

Thank You Lord that it is written that they will prosper and be in health, just as their souls prosper. In the name of Jesus Christ.

3 John 1:2

Thank You Lord that every plant which their heavenly Father has not planted shall be rooted up. In the name of Jesus Christ.

Matthew 15:13

Thank You Lord that You will feel compassion for them and heal those who are sick. In the name of Jesus Christ.

Matthew 14:14

Thank You Lord that if they forgive men for their transgressions, their heavenly Father will also forgive them. In the name of Jesus Christ.

Matthew 6:14

This is a key to healing – that they will not harbor any unforgiveness.

Oh Lord my God, Thank You that they cried to You for help, and You healed them. Oh Lord You have brought their soul from Sheol (death). You have kept them alive that they should not go down to the pit. In the name of Jesus Christ.

Psalm 30:2-3

Thank You Lord that they are freed from their sickness. In the name of Jesus Christ.

Luke 13:12

Thank You Lord that You sent Your Word and healed them, and delivered them from their destruction. In the name of Jesus Christ.

Psalm 107:20

Thank You Lord that You will have compassion on the afflicted. In the name of Jesus Christ.

Isaiah 49:13

Thank You Lord that the eyes of the blind will be opened, and the ears of the deaf will be unstopped. In the name of Jesus Christ.

Isaiah 35:5

Thank You Lord that the lame will leap like the deer, and the tongues of the dumb will shout for joy. In the name of Jesus Christ.

Isaiah 35:6

Thank You Lord that they will bless the Lord with all their soul, and forget none of His benefits: He pardons all their iniquities, He heals all their diseases. In the name of Jesus Christ.

Psalm 103:3

Thank You Lord that they will not be wise in their own eyes: they will fear the Lord, and turn away from evil. It will be healing to their body, and refreshment to their bones. In the name of Jesus Christ.

Proverbs 3:7

Thank You Lord that we bring to You many who are demon possessed: and You will cast out the spirits with a word, and heal all those who are ill, in order that what was spoken through Isaiah the prophet might be fulfilled saying, 'He Himself took their infirmities and carried away their diseases.' In the name of Jesus Christ.

Matthew 8:16-17

Thank You Lord that You will come and heal them. In the name of Jesus Christ.

Matthew 8:7

Thank You Lord that by Your holy stripes they are healed. In the name of Jesus Christ.

Isaiah 53:5

Thank You Lord that You have set the captives free and they are free indeed. In the name of Jesus Christ.

Isaiah 61:1

Thank You Lord that You will sustain them upon their sickbed. In their illness You will restore them to health. In the name of Jesus Christ.

Psalm 41:3

Thank You Lord that they shall not die, but live to tell of the works of the Lord. In the name of Jesus Christ.

Psalm 118.17

Thank You Lord that the power of the Lord is present for Jesus to perform healing. In the name of Jesus Christ.

Luke 5:17

Thank You Lord that their faith has made them well; they may go in peace, and be healed of their affliction. In the name of Jesus Christ.

Mark 5:34

Thank You Lord that great multitudes come to You, bringing with them those who are lame, crippled, blind, dumb, and many others, and they lay them down at Your feet; and You heal them and they will marvel as they see the dumb speaking, the cripple restored, and the lame walking and the blind seeing, and they will glorify the God of Israel. In the name of Jesus Christ.

Matthew 15:30

Thank You Lord that when You stand over them and rebuke the fever it will leave them. In the name of Jesus Christ.

Luke 4:39

Thank You Lord that You have done all things well. You make even the deaf to hear, and the dumb to speak. In the name of Jesus Christ.

Mark 7:37

Thank You Lord that they will destroy speculations and every lofty thing raised up against the knowledge of God, and they will take every thought captive to the obedience of Christ. In the name of Jesus Christ.

2 Corinthians 10:5

Thank You Lord that those who believe in You, the works that You did, *they shall do also* and even greater works than what Jesus did they shall do, because You are with the Father, and *whatever they ask in Your name, that will You do*, that the Father may be glorified in the Son. In the name of Jesus Christ.

John 14:11-14

Thank You Lord that on the basis of faith in Jesus' name, it is the name of Jesus which has strengthened these people whom You see and know; and the faith which comes through Him has given these people this perfect health in the presence of you all. In the name of Jesus Christ.

Acts 3:16

Thank You Lord that You have told us this is the sign of believers, that they lay hands on the sick and they shall recover. In the name of Jesus Christ.

Mark 16:18

Thank You Lord that the prayer offered in faith will restore the one who is sick. In the name of Jesus Christ.

James 5:15

Thank You Lord that You will heal every kind of disease and every kind of sickness among these people. Thank You Lord that we, as intercessors, will bring to You all who are ill, taken with various diseases, and pains, demoniacs, epileptics, paralytics, and You will heal them. In the name of Jesus Christ.

Matthew 4:23-24

Thank You Lord that You will restore them because You have compassion on them. In the name of Jesus Christ.

Zechariah 10:6

Thank You Lord that they will turn to God in repentance and have faith in the Lord Jesus Christ. In the name of Jesus Christ.

Acts 20:21

Thank You Lord that they believe that You are the God who gives life to the dead, and calls into being that which does not exist. In the name of Jesus Christ.

Romans 4:17

Thank You Lord that You have seen their ways, but You will heal them, and lead them, and restore comfort to them and to their mourners In the name of Jesus Christ.

Isaiah 57:18

Thank You Lord that You will anoint us with the Holy Spirit and with power, and we will go about doing good, and healing all who are oppressed by the devil; for You are with us. In the name of Jesus Christ.

Acts 10:38

Thank You Lord that You have heard their prayer, You have seen their tears, behold You will heal them. On the third day they will go up to the house of the Lord. In the name of Jesus Christ.

2 Kings 20:5

Thank You Lord that all things they ask in prayer, believing, they shall receive. In the name of Jesus Christ.

Matthew 21:22

Thank You Lord that when they are brought to You, You heal all who are ill. In the name of Jesus Christ

Matthew 8:16

Thank You Lord that they cry to You for help and You will heal them. In the name of Jesus Christ.

Psalm 30:2

Thank You Lord that You will say to them 'receive your sight; your faith has made you well,' and they will regain their sight. In the name of Jesus Christ.

Luke 18:42

Thank You Lord that You are the God that heals. In the name of Jesus Christ.

Exodus 15:26

Thank You Lord that You fill us with good things so our youth is renewed like the eagle's. In the name of Jesus Christ.

Psalm 103:5

Thank You Lord, oh Lord my God, that You will let my/their sight return. In the name of Jesus Christ.

1 Kings 17:22

Thank You Lord that You will restore all of us to health and heal our wounds. In the name of Jesus Christ.

Jeremiah 30:17

Thank You Lord that You will say to the dead, "get up!" And the dead will sit up and begin to talk. In the name of Jesus Christ.

Luke 7:14-15

Thank You Lord that the blind receive sight, the lame walk, those who have leprosy are cured, the deaf hear, the dead are raised, and the good news is preached to the poor. In the name of Jesus Christ.

Luke 7:22

Thank You Lord that You are the God who performs miracles; thank You that You display Your power among the people. In the name of Jesus Christ.

Psalm 77:14

Thank You Lord that You will keep us from every disease. In the name of Jesus Christ.

Deuteronomy 7:15

Thank You Lord that You are the strength of my heart. In the name of Jesus Christ.

Psalm 73:26

Thank You Lord that You will revive us/them according to your loving kindness so that we/they may keep the testimonies of Your Mouth. In the name of Jesus Christ.

Psalm 119:88

Thank You Lord! Jesus Christ heals you! In the name of Jesus Christ.

Acts 9:34

Adoni-Rofekha!

DELIVERANCE

For those who doubt God, for the depressed, oppressed, suicidal, for the alcohol or drug addicted, for those suffering from mental difficulties, from childhood traumas, incest, child abuse; for those in occult activity, and for those involved in dishonest, immoral, criminal or violent activities.

Thank You Lord that all these people/we will repent and return, that their/our sins may be wiped away, in order that times of refreshing may come from the presence of the Lord; and that You may send Jesus the Christ appointed for them/us. In the name of Jesus Christ.

Act 3:19-20

Thank You Lord that all these people will repent and believe in the Gospel. In the name of Jesus Christ.

Mark 1:15

Thank You Lord that all of these people will submit to God. They will resist the devil and he will flee from them. They will draw near to God and God will draw near to them. Cleanse your hands, you sinners, and purify your hearts you double minded. In the name of Jesus Christ.

James 4:7-8

Thank You Lord that You may grant these people repentance, leading to the knowledge of the truth, and that they may come to their senses and escape from the snare of the devil, having been held captive by him to do his will. In the name of Jesus Christ.

2 Timothy 2:25-26

Thank You Lord that because of the tender mercy of our God, with which the Sunrise from on high shall visit them, to shine upon those who sit in darkness and the shadow of death, to guide their feet into the way of peace. In the name of Jesus Christ.

Luke 1:78-79

Thank You Lord that You said 'Light shall shine out of darkness', and You are the one who has shone in these people's hearts to give the light of the knowledge of the glory of God in the face of Christ. In the name of Jesus Christ.

2 Corinthians 4:6

Thank You Lord that the blood of Christ will cleanse their conscience from dead works to serve the living God. In the name of Jesus Christ.

Hebrews 9:14

Thank You Lord that each one of these people will repent, and each one of them will be baptized in the name of Jesus Christ for forgiveness of their sins: and they shall receive the gift of the Holy Spirit. For the promise is for them and their children, and for all who are far off, as many as the Lord our God shall call to Himself may they be saved from this perverse generation. In the name of Jesus Christ.

Act 2:38-40

Thank You Lord that they having the promises of God cleanse themselves from all defilement of flesh and spirit, perfecting holiness in the fear of God. In the name of Jesus Christ.

2 Corinthians 7:1

Thank You Lord that there is no condemnation for those who are in Christ Jesus. For the law of the Spirit of life in Christ Jesus has set them free from the law of sin and of death. In the name of Jesus Christ.

Romans 8:1-2

Thank You Lord that they will know that they have come to know You, if they keep Your commandments. The one that says, 'I have come to know Him', and does not keep Your commandments, is a liar, and the truth is not in him: but whoever keeps Your Word, in these people the love of God has truly been perfected. By this they will know that they are in You. In the name of Jesus Christ.

I John 2:3-5

Thank You Lord for delivering them from the domain of darkness and transferring them to the kingdom of Your beloved Son, in whom we have redemption and the forgiveness of sins. In the name of Jesus Christ.

Colossians 1:13-14

Thank You Lord that they should repent, and turn to God performing deeds appropriate to repentance. In the name of Jesus Christ.

Acts 26:20

Thank You Lord that Your kindness will lead them to repentance. In the name of Jesus Christ.

Romans 2:4

Thank You Lord that You will direct their hearts into the love of God and into the steadfastness of Christ. In the name of Jesus Christ.

2 Thessalonians 3:5

Thank You Lord that the Son of God appeared for this purpose, that He might destroy the works of the devil in the lives of these people. In the name of Jesus Christ.

1 John 3:8

Thank You Lord that as far as the east is from the west, so far have You removed their transgressions from them. In the name of Jesus Christ.

Psalm 103:12

Thank You Lord that You will rescue their lives from oppression and violence. In the name of Jesus Christ.

Psalm 72:14

Thank You Lord that You will open their eyes so that they may turn from darkness to light and from the dominion of satan to God, in order that they may receive forgiveness of sins, and an inheritance among those who have been sanctified by faith in Jesus. In the name of Jesus Christ.

Acts 26:18

Thank You Lord that You will put away from them a deceitful mouth, and put devious lips far from them. In the name of Jesus Christ.

Proverbs 4:24

Thank You Lord that You laugh at the wicked, he knows his day is coming. The power of the wicked will be broken. In the name of Jesus Christ.

Psalm 37:13,17

Thank You Lord that You will deliver them from all of their transgressions; make them not the reproach of the foolish. In the name of Jesus Christ.

Psalm 39:8

Thank You Lord that they will fear the Lord, and hate evil. In the name of Jesus Christ.

Proverbs 8:13

Thank You Lord that they abstain from sexual immorality, for it is Your will for their sanctification. In the name of Jesus Christ.

1 Thessalonians 4:3

Thank You Lord that You will wash them thoroughly from any iniquity and cleanse them from their sin. In the name of Jesus Christ.

Psalm 51:2

Thank You Lord that they are transformed by the renewing of their minds. In the name of Jesus Christ.

Romans 12:2

Thank You Lord for treading their iniquities underfoot and casting all their sins into the depths of the sea. In the name of Jesus Christ.

Micah 7:19

Thank You Lord for delivering them from the hand of the wicked. In the name of Jesus Christ.

Psalm 97:10

Thank You Lord that when the righteous cry, You hear them and deliver them out of all their troubles. In the name of Jesus Christ.

Psalm 34:17

Thank You Lord for putting a new song in their mouths, a song of praise to our God. Many will see and fear, and will trust in the Lord. In the name of Jesus Christ.

Psalm 40:3

Thank You Lord that those who have been troubled with unclean spirits are being cured. In the name of Jesus Christ.

Luke 6:18

Thank You Lord that You are reconciling all these people through the blood of Christ to Yourself. In the name of Jesus Christ.

2 Corinthians 5:18

Thank You Lord that You have not destined them for wrath, but for obtaining salvation through our Lord Jesus Christ. In the name of Jesus Christ.

1 Thessalonians 5:9

Thank You Lord that You have sent Jesus to proclaim release to the captives. In the name of Jesus Christ.

Luke 4:8

Thank You Lord that the God of peace will soon crush satan under their feet. In the name of Jesus Christ.

Romans 16:20

Thank You Lord that You help them and deliver them, because they take refuge in You. In the name of Jesus Christ.

Psalm 37:40

Thank You Lord that You will speak peace to Your people, to Your godly ones, but let them not turn back in folly. In the name of Jesus Christ.

Psalm 85:8

Unforgiveness opens a doorway for satan

Thank You Lord that if they forgive men their transgressions, their heavenly Father will also forgive them. In the name of Jesus Christ.

Matthew 6:14

Thank You Lord for bringing them out of the pit of destruction, out of the miry clay, and for setting their feet upon a rock, making their footsteps firm. In the name of Jesus Christ.

Psalm 40:2

Thank You Lord for redeeming their lives from the pit, and crowning them with loving kindness and compassion. In the name of Jesus Christ.

Psalm 103:4

Thank You Lord that they will obey Your voice, and You will be their God, and they will be Your people, and they will walk in all the ways in which You command them, that it may be well with them. In the name of Jesus Christ.

Jeremiah 7:23

Thank You Lord that they will depart from evil, and do good; they seek peace and pursue it. In the name of Jesus Christ.

Psalm 34:14

Thank You Lord that You will deliver them from the hand of the wicked, and You will redeem them from the grasp of the violent. In the name of Jesus Christ.

Jeremiah 15:21

Thank You Lord that the wicked will forsake his way and the unrighteous man his thoughts; thank You Lord that they will return to You, and You will have compassion on them, and to their God for You will abundantly pardon. In the name of Jesus Christ.

Isaiah 55:7

Thank You Lord that their souls have escaped as a bird out of the snare of the trapper, the snare is broken and they have escaped. In the name of Jesus Christ.

Psalm 124:7

Thank You Lord that You will turn the curse into a blessing for us because You love us. In the name of Jesus Christ.

Deuteronomy 23:5

Thank You Lord that they cried out to You in their trouble; and You delivered them out of their distresses. In the name of Jesus Christ.

Psalm 107:6

Thank You Lord that You look upon their affliction and their trouble, and forgive all their sins. In the name of Jesus Christ.

Psalm 25:18

Thank You Lord that they will walk in the way of good men, and keep the paths of the righteous. In the name of Jesus Christ.

Proverbs 2:20

Thank You Lord that You will deliver them from every evil deed, and You will bring them safely to Your heavenly Kingdom. In the name of Jesus Christ.

2 Timothy 4:18

Thank You Lord that You have been saying to them, come out of them, you unclean spirit. In the name of Jesus Christ.

Mark 5:8

Thank You Lord for rebuking the unclean spirit, saying to it, 'You deaf and dumb spirit, I command you, come out of them, and do not enter them again.' In the name of Jesus Christ.

Mark 9:25

Thank You Lord that even the demons are subject to us in Your name. In the name of Jesus Christ.

Luke 10:17

Thank You Lord that they may be delivered from perverse and evil men. In the name of Jesus Christ.

2 Thessalonians 3:2

Thank You Lord that they will draw near with a sincere heart in full assurance of faith. Thank You Lord that they are having their hearts sprinkled clean from an evil conscience and their bodies washed with pure water. In the name of Jesus Christ.

Hebrews 10:22

Thank You Lord that they are destroying speculation and every lofty thing raised up against the knowledge of God, and they are taking every thought captive to the obedience of Christ. In the name of Jesus Christ.

2 Corinthians 10:5

Thank You Lord that the enemy will not deceive them nor the son of wickedness afflict them. You will crush their adversaries before them and strike those who hate them. In the name of Jesus Christ.

Psalm 89:22-23

Thank You Lord that You will purge the evil from among us. In the name of Jesus Christ.

Deuteronomy 19:19

Thank You Lord that You have given us authority to tread upon serpents and scorpions and over all the power of the enemy and nothing shall injure us. In the name of Jesus Christ.

Luke 10:19

Thank You Lord that by Your death, You might render powerless him who had the power of death - that is the devil; and might deliver those who through fear of death were subject to slavery all their lives. In the name of Jesus Christ.

Hebrews 2:14-15

Thank You Lord that You cast out their demons. In the name of Jesus Christ.

Mark 1:34

Thank You Lord that these people will not be overcome with evil, but will overcome evil with good. In the name of Jesus Christ.

Romans 12:21

Thank You Lord that to You belong compassion and forgiveness, for we have rebelled against You. In the name of Jesus Christ.

Daniel 9:9

Thank You Lord that if we confess our sins, He is faithful and righteous to forgive us our sins and to cleanse us from all unrighteousness. In the name of Jesus Christ.

1 John 1:9

Thank You Lord that they will be filled with the knowledge of God's will in all spiritual wisdom and understanding. In the name of Jesus Christ.

Colossians 1:9

Thank You Lord that just as Christ was raised from the dead through the glory of the Father, we/they too may have new life. In the name of Jesus Christ.

Romans 6:4

Thank You Lord that You will direct my footsteps according to Your Word. Thank You Lord that You will let no sin rule over us/them. In the name of Jesus Christ.

Psalm 119:133

Thank You Lord that You will turn our/their eyes away from worthless things and You will preserve our/their life according to Your Word. In the name of Jesus Christ.

Psalm 119:33

Thank You Lord that we have considered our ways and have turned our/their steps to Your statues. In the name of Jesus Christ.

Psalm 119:59

Thank You Lord that we/they will repent and we/they will turn away from all our offenses, then sin will not be our downfall. Thank

SCRIPTURAL PRAYERS FOR DELIVERANCE

You that we will rid ourselves of all our offenses we have committed against You and get a new heart and a new spirit – we will <u>repent</u> and <u>live</u>. In the name of Jesus Christ.

Ezekiel 18:30-32

RELATIONSHIPS

Thank You Lord that their/our love is perfect for each other, and has **no fear** - no fear of being judged, criticized, controlled, abandoned, rejected, or being shamed. In the name of Jesus Christ.

1 John 4:18

Thank You Lord that they will all be harmonious, sympathetic, brotherly, kindhearted, and humble in spirit; not returning evil for evil, or insult for insult, but giving a blessing instead, for they were called for the very purpose that they might inherit a blessing. In the name of Jesus Christ.

1 Peter 3:8

Thank You Lord that they will be devoted to one another in brotherly love; giving preference to one another in honor; not lagging behind in diligence, fervent in spirit, serving the Lord; rejoicing in hope, persevering in tribulation, devoted to prayer, contributing to the needs of the saints, practicing hospitality. In the name of Jesus Christ.

Romans 12:10-13

Thank You Lord that You who give perseverance and encouragement will grant them to be of the same mind with one another according to Christ Jesus; that with one accord they may with one voice glorify the God and Father of our Lord Jesus Christ. In the name of Jesus Christ.

Romans 15:5-6

Thank You Lord that they will be able to speak with their mouths what fills their hearts. In the name of Jesus Christ.

Luke 6:45

Thank You Lord that You will make their joy complete by making them be of the same mind, maintaining the same love, united in spirit, and intent on the same purpose. In the name of Jesus Christ.

Philippians 2:2

Thank You Lord that they will put aside all anger, wrath, malice, slander, and abusive speech from their mouths. They do not lie to one another since they have laid aside the old self with its evil practices. In the name of Jesus Christ.

Colossians 3:8-9

Thank You Lord that You will cause them to increase and abound in love for one another and for all men just as we also do for You, so that You may establish their hearts blameless in holiness before our God and Father. In the name of Jesus Christ.

1 Thessalonians 3:12-13

Thank You Lord that their hearts may be encouraged, having been knit together in love. In the name of Jesus Christ.

Colossians 2:2

Thank You Lord that they will speak to each other all that is in their hearts. In the name of Jesus Christ.

2 Chronicles 9:1

Thank You Lord that they will forgive each other their transgressions, so that their heavenly Father will forgive them. In the name of Jesus Christ.

Matthew 6:14

Thank You Lord that they let all bitterness and wrath and anger and brawling and slander be put away from them, along with all malice. Thank You Lord that they are kind to one another, tenderhearted, forgiving each other, just as God in Christ also has forgiven them. In the name of Jesus Christ.

Ephesians 4:31-32

Thank You Lord that they will walk in a manner worthy of the calling with which they have been called, with all humility and gentleness, with patience, showing forbearance to one another in love. Being diligent to preserve the unity of the Spirit in the bond of peace. In the name of Jesus Christ.

Ephesians 4:1-3

Thank You Lord that You are the Lord of their peace and You have made them one, and You have broken down the barrier of the dividing wall. In the name of Jesus Christ.

Ephesians 2:14

Thank You Lord that these people follow Your commandment to love one another just as You have loved them. In the name of Jesus Christ.

John 15:12

Thank You Lord that they let no root of bitterness spring up between them to cause trouble. In the name of Jesus Christ.

Hebrews 12:15

Thank You Lord that they will live in harmony in the Lord. In the name of Jesus Christ.

Philippians 4:2

Thank You Lord that You are reconciling all these people through the blood of Christ to Yourself, and to each other. In the name of Jesus Christ.

2 Corinthians 5:19

Thank You Lord that the wife will be subject to her husband, as is fitting in the Lord. In the name of Jesus Christ.

Colossians 3:18

Thank You Lord that the husband will love his wife, and not be embittered against her. In the name of Jesus Christ.

Colossians 3:19

Thank You Lord that they abstain from sexual immorality for it is Your will for their sanctification. In the name of Jesus Christ.

1 Thessalonians 4:3

Thank You Lord that the wife is the husband's beloved, and his desire is for his wife and the wife's desire is for her husband. In the name of Jesus Christ.

Solomon 7:10

Thank You Lord that children will be obedient to their parents in all things, for this is pleasing to You. In the name of Jesus Christ.

Colossians 3:20

Thank You Lord that You may cause them to increase and abound in love for one another and for all men. In the name of Jesus Christ.

1 Thessalonians 3:12

Thank You Lord that they will love one another, for love is from God, and everyone who loves is born of God and knows God. In the name of Jesus Christ.

1 John 4:7

Thank You Lord that no weapon formed against this relationship will prosper. In the name of Jesus Christ.

Isaiah 54:17

Thank You Lord that You make up to them for the years that the swarming locusts have eaten. In the name of Jesus Christ.

Joel 2:25

Thank You Lord that these people will not love with word or with tongue, but in deed and truth. They will know by this that they are of the truth, and their hearts shall be assured before You. In the name of Jesus Christ.

1 John 3:18-19

Thank You Lord that they will agree, and there will be no division among them, but that they will be made complete in the same mind and the same judgment. In the name of Jesus Christ.

1 Corinthians 1:10

Thank You Lord that the husbands will love the wives just as Christ also loved the Church and gave Himself up for Her. In the name of Jesus Christ.

Ephesians 5:25

Thank You Lord that You will be a wall of fire around their marriage and/or their relationship, and You will be the glory in their midst. In the name of Jesus Christ.

Zechariah 2:5

Thank You Lord that no lies will be found in their mouths. In the name of Jesus Christ.

Zephaniah 3:13

Thank You Lord, that he who finds a wife finds a good thing, and he will obtain favor from the Lord. In the name of Jesus Christ.

Proverbs 18:22

Thank You Lord that it is You who blesses the righteous man, You surround his marriage and/or relationship as with a shield. In the name of Jesus Christ.

Psalm 5:12

Thank You Lord that You will restore the hearts of the fathers to their children, and the hearts of the children to their fathers, lest You come and smite the land with a curse. In the name of Jesus Christ.

Malachi 4:6

Thank You Lord that they will rejoice, be made complete, be comforted, be like minded, live in peace, and the God of love and peace shall be with them. In the name of Jesus Christ.

2 Corinthians 13:11

Thank You Lord that these people will bear with one another, and forgive each other whoever has a complaint against anyone; just as the Lord forgave them, so they also should forgive each other, and beyond all these things put on love, which is the perfect bond of unity, and let the peace of Christ rule in their hearts, to which indeed they were called in one body, and be thankful. In the name of Jesus Christ.

Colossians 3:13-15

Thank You Lord that they are destroying speculation and every lofty thing raised up against the knowledge of God, and taking every thought captive to the obedience of Christ in their relationship. In the name of Jesus Christ.

2 Corinthians 10:5

Thank You Lord that for those who are married, let their marriages be held in honor among all, and let their marriage bed be undefiled, for fornicators and adulterers God will judge. In the name of Jesus Christ.

Hebrews 13:4

Thank You Lord that they will pursue the things which make for peace and the building up of one another. In the name of Jesus Christ.

Romans 14:19

Thank You Lord that You will take of the Spirit who is upon me and place it on them: and they shall bear the burden of the people with me, so that I shall not bear it alone. In the name of Jesus Christ.

Numbers 11:17

Thank You Lord that they are standing firm in one spirit, with one mind striving together for the faith of the gospel. In the name of Jesus Christ.

Philippians 1:27

Thank You Lord that at the beginning of creation you made male and female. For this reason a man will leave his father and mother and be united to his wife, and the two will become one flesh. Thank You Lord that they are no longer two, but one. Therefore what You God have joined together, let no man separate. In the name of Jesus Christ.

Mark 10:6-9

WISDOM AND GUIDANCE

'The fear of the Lord is the beginning of Wisdom. Fools despise wisdom and instruction.'

Proverbs 1:7

The fear of the Lord leads to life; then one rests content, untouched by trouble. In the name of Jesus Christ.

Proverbs 19:23

Thank You Lord that the Holy Spirit will lead them/us into all truth. In the name of Jesus Christ.

John 16:13

Thank You Lord that You will sanctify us in the truth. Your Word is truth. In the name of Jesus Christ.

John 17:17

Thank You Lord that You will open our minds to understand scripture. In the name of Jesus Christ.

Luke 24:45

Thank You Lord that we will do everything You have said – we will obey! In the name of Jesus Christ.

Exodus 24:7

Thank You Lord that You will make us know Your ways, Oh Lord teach us Your paths. Lead us in Your truth and teach us, for You are the God of our salvation; for You, we wait all day. In the name of Jesus Christ.

Psalm 25:4-5

Thank You Lord that as the angel of God, so we shall be, to discern good and evil. And may the Lord our God be with us. In the name of Jesus Christ.

2 Samuel 14:17

Thank You Lord that we will not be conformed to this world, but we are transformed by the renewing of our mind, that we may prove what the will of God is, that which is good and acceptable and perfect. In the name of Jesus Christ.

Romans 12:2

Thank You Lord that You will reach out and touch our mouths, and say to us, 'Behold I have put My words into your mouth.' In the name of Jesus Christ.

Jeremiah 1:9

Thank You Lord that You store up sound wisdom for us. You are a shield to us who walk in integrity. In the name of Jesus Christ.

Proverbs 2:7

Thank You Lord that I have considered my ways and have turned my steps to Your statues. In the name of Jesus Christ.

Psalm 119:59

Thank You Lord that You have given us the tongues of disciples, that we may know how to sustain the weary one with a word. You awaken us morning by morning. You awaken our ear to listen as disciples. You have opened our ears and, we are not disobedient, nor do we turn back. In the name of Jesus Christ.

Isaiah 50:4-5

Thank You Lord that we will be wise in what is good and innocent in what is evil, and You, the God of peace, will soon crush satan under our feet. In the name of Jesus Christ.

Romans 16:19-20

Thank You Lord that we will fear the Lord. You will instruct us in the way we should choose. Our souls will abide in prosperity, and our descendants will inherit the land. In the name of Jesus Christ.

Psalm 25:12-13

Thank You Lord that You will give us one heart and one way, that we may fear You always for our own good and the good of our children. And You will make an everlasting covenant with us that You will not turn away from us, to do us good. In the name of Jesus Christ.

Jeremiah 32:39-40

Thank You Lord that You, the God of our Lord Jesus Christ, the Father of glory may give us a spirit of wisdom and of revelation in the knowledge of Him. In the name of Jesus Christ.

Ephesians 1:17

Thank You Lord that You will fill us with a knowledge of Your will in all spiritual wisdom and understanding, so that we may walk in a manner worthy of the Lord, to please You in all respects, bearing fruit in every good work and increasing in the knowledge of God. In the name of Jesus Christ.

Colossians 1:9-10

Thank You Lord that You will be the stability of our times, a wealth of salvation, wisdom, and knowledge; the fear of the Lord is our treasure. In the name of Jesus Christ.

Isaiah 33:6

Thank You Lord that we will all have the mind of Christ. In the name of Jesus Christ.

1 Corinthians 3:16

Thank You Lord that You will give us a mind that understands and eyes that see and ears that hear. In the name of Jesus Christ.

Deuteronomy 29:4

Thank You Lord that You will grant unto us to know the mysteries of the Kingdom of heaven. In the name of Jesus Christ.

Matthew 13:11

Thank You Lord that You will instruct us and teach us the way in which we should go, You will counsel us with Your eye upon us. In the name of Jesus Christ.

Psalm 32:8

Thank You Lord that we will seek first the kingdom of God and Your righteousness, and all these things shall be added unto us. In the name of Jesus Christ.

Matthew 6:33

Thank You Lord that You will speak, for Your servant is listening. In the name of Jesus Christ.

Thank You Lord that You open our ear to instruction, and command that we return from evil. In the name of Jesus Christ.

Job 36:10

Thank You Lord that You will teach us great discernment and knowledge. In the name of Jesus Christ.

Psalm 119:66

Thank You Lord that You have counselled us. Indeed our mind instructs us in the night. In the name of Jesus Christ.

Psalm 16:7

Thank You Lord that You will bless us with insight and we will shine brightly like the brightness of the expanse of Heaven, and we will lead many to righteousness like the stars forever and ever. In the name of Jesus Christ.

Daniel 12:3

Thank You Lord that You will give us utterance and wisdom which none of our opponents will be able to resist or refute. In the name of Jesus Christ.

Luke 21:15

Thank You Lord that the Spirit of the Lord will rest upon us. The Spirit of wisdom, understanding, counsel, strength, knowledge, and the fear of the Lord. In the name of Jesus Christ.

Isaiah 11:2

Thank You Lord that You desire truth in our innermost being, and in our hidden part, You will make us know wisdom. In the name of Jesus Christ.

Psalm 51:6

Thank You Lord that You teach us Your paths. In the name of Jesus Christ.

Psalm 25:4

Thank You Lord that our mouths will speak wisdom; and the meditation of our hearts will be understanding. In the name of Jesus Christ.

Psalm 49:3

Thank You Lord that You will continually guide us, and satisfy our desire in scorched places, and give strength to our bones, and we will be like a watered garden, and like a spring of water whose waters do not fail. In the name of Jesus Christ.

Isaiah 58:11

Thank You Lord that You will give us understanding in everything. In the name of Jesus Christ.

2 Timothy 2:7

Thank You Lord that if any of us lacks wisdom, we will ask of You, Who gives to all men generously and without reproach, and it will be given to us. In the name of Jesus Christ.

James 1:5

Thank You Lord that You will go before us and make our rough places smooth. You will shatter the doors of bronze, and cut through our iron bars. In the name of Jesus Christ.

Isaiah 45:2

Thank You Lord that our mouths utter wisdom, and our tongues speak justice. Thank You Lord that the law of God is in our hearts, and we do not slip. In the name of Jesus Christ.

Psalm 37:30-31

Thank You Lord that we will obey Your voice, and You will be our God, and we will be Your people; and we will walk in all the way which You command us, that it may be well with us. In the name of Jesus Christ.

Jeremiah 7:23

Thank You Lord that we will acquire wisdom, and with all our acquiring, we will get understanding. In the name of Jesus Christ.

Proverbs 4:7

Thank You Lord that You will give us the treasures of darkness, and hidden wealth of secret places, in order that we may know that it is You the Lord, the God of Israel, who calls us by our name. In the name of Jesus Christ.

Isaiah 45:3

Thank You Lord that we are on the path of life, and we heed Your instruction. In the name of Jesus Christ.

Proverbs 10:17

Thank You Lord that through You we will push back our adversaries. Through Your name we will trample down those who rise up against us. In the name of Jesus Christ.

Psalm 44:5

Thank You Lord that we love discipline and we love knowledge. In the name of Jesus Christ.

Proverbs 12:1

Thank You Lord that the foot of pride will not come upon us, and the hand of the wicked will not drive us away. In the name of Jesus Christ.

Psalm 36:11

Thank You Lord that our tongue will be like the pen of a ready writer, grace will be poured out upon our lips. In the name of Jesus Christ.

Psalm 45:1-2

Thank You Lord that You will send out Your light and Your truth and they will lead us. In the name of Jesus Christ.

Psalm 43:3

Thank You Lord that we will fear the Lord and turn away from evil. In the name of Jesus Christ.

Proverbs 3:7

Thank You Lord that we will know the wisdom from above which is first pure, then peaceable, gentle, reasonable, full of mercy and good fruits, unwavering, without hypocrisy. In the name of Jesus Christ.

James 3:17

Thank You Lord that we will keep sound wisdom and discernment. In the name of Jesus Christ.

Proverbs 3:21

Thank You Lord that You will reveal deep and hidden things. You Oh Lord know what lies in darkness and light dwells with You. In the name of Jesus Christ.

Daniel 2:22

Thank You Lord that wisdom will enter our hearts and knowledge will be pleasant to our soul; discretion will protect us, and under-standing will guard us. In the name of Jesus Christ.

Proverbs 2:10-11

Thank You Lord that we/they will repent, You will restore us/them that we/they may serve You; thank You that if we/ they utter worthy words, not worthless words, we/they will be Your spokesman. Let the people turn to us/them but we/ they will not turn to them. In the name of Jesus Christ.

Jeremiah 15:20

Thank You Lord that You will set a guard over our mouths; Oh Lord I Thank You that You will keep watch over our/ their lips. Let not their/our hearts be drawn to evil to take part in evil deeds with men who are evil doers. In the name of Jesus Christ.

Psalm 141:3

Thank You Lord that You will give us/them insight and understanding. In the name Jesus Christ.

2 Timothy 2:7

Thank You Lord that Your angels will touch our mouths and we will begin to speak. In the name of Jesus Christ.

Daniel 10:16

Thank You Lord that You will teach us Your way, and we will walk in Your truth. Thank You that You will give us an undivided heart that we may fear Your name. In the name of Jesus Christ.

Psalm 86:11

Thank You Lord that the Spirit of God is in us and we have insight, intelligence, and outstanding wisdom. In the name of Jesus Christ.

Daniel 5:14

Thank You Lord that You will teach us/them knowledge and good judgement for we believe in Your commandments. In the name of Jesus Christ.

Psalm 119:67

Speak lord, for your servant is listening. In the name of Jesus Christ!!!

Daniel 5:14

Thank You Lord that we and all of our family are devout and God fearing: We give generously to those in need and pray regularly to God. In the name of Jesus Christ.

Acts 10:2

Thank You Lord that we all realize how true it is that God does not show favoritism but accepts men from every Nation who fear Him and do what is right. In the name of Jesus Christ.

Acts 10:34

Thank You Lord that no one can stand up against our wisdom or the Spirit by whom we speak. In the name of Jesus Christ.

Acts 6:16

Thank You Lord that I desire to do Your will Oh my God. Your law is written in my heart. In the name of Jesus Christ.

Psalm 40:8

Thank You Lord that we will be full of the Spirit and wisdom and we will give ourselves to prayer and ministry of the Word. In the name of Jesus Christ.

Acts 6:3-4

Thank You Lord that we will obey God rather than men. In the name of Jesus Christ.

Acts 5:20

Thank You Lord that in the past You have overlooked ignorance but now You call people everywhere to repent. Thank You that You have set a day when You will judge the world with justice by the Man You have appointed. Thank You Lord that You have given proof of this to all men by raising Him from the dead. In the name of Jesus Christ.

Acts 17:30-31

Thank You Lord that You will bring all work into judgement. Including every secret thing whether good or evil. In the name of Jesus Christ.

Ecclesiastes 12:14

Thank You Lord that You tell us to keep Your Sabbaths holy, that there may be a sign between us. Then we will know that You are the Lord our God. In the name of Jesus Christ.

Ezekiel 20:20

Thank You Lord and praise You Lord, oh God of our fathers, for You have given us/them wisdom and power and made known to us what we ask of You. In the name of Jesus Christ.

Daniel 2:20

Thank You Lord that when we speak, we will speak with wisdom and tact. In the name of Jesus Christ.

Daniel 2:14

Thank You Lord that like You oh Lord, we/they will speak righteousness, and we/they will speak what is right. In the name of Jesus Christ.

Isaiah 45:19

Thank You Lord that we will stop judging by mere appearances, and make a right judgement. In the name of Jesus Christ.

John 7:24

Thank You Lord that we will not lean on our own understanding, but we will trust the Lord with all our might and He will direct our paths. In the name of Jesus Christ.

Proverbs 3:5-6

The Ten Commandments are simply God's instructions for righteousness and the fulfillment of the abundant life. God loves each and every soul on this earth so much, that He is giving these instructions for our well being. These commandments keep us safe, healthy, happy and peaceful. When we rebel against God's commandments, we ourselves open a doorway to misery!!! However, because of The Lord's tender mercy, He is always waiting for reconciliation. He longs for divine union with us. This divine union and reconciliation can only come through repentance. The Lord speaks of repentance throughout the scriptures. "Repent, and believe in the Gospel" "Repent or you will all perish!" "Repent and live!" 'Turn from your wicked ways (repent) and I will HEAL THE LAND"!

Thank You Lord that if we confess our sins, You are faithful and righteous to forgive us our sins and cleanse us from all unrighteousness. In the name of Jesus Christ.

1 John I:9

Thank You Lord that You command us to love one another. As You have loved us, so we must love one another. By this all men will know that we are Your disciples if we love one another. In the name of Jesus Christ.

John 13:34

***"To believe is to obey God. Faith itself is
obedience, but faith also produces obedience."***

GOD COMMANDS

- *Thank You Lord that we will have no other Gods before You.*

- *Thank You Lord that we will not make for ourselves an idol in the form of anything in heaven above or on the earth beneath or in the waters below.*

- *Thank You Lord that we shall not bow down to them or worship them; for You the Lord our God are a jealous God, punishing the children for the sins of the fathers to the third and fourth generation of those who hate You, but showing love to a thousand generations of those who love You and keep Your commandments.*

- *Thank You Lord that we shall not misuse the name of the Lord our God, for the Lord will not hold anyone guiltless who misuses His Name.*

- *Thank You Lord that we will remember the Sabbath to keep it holy, six days we will labor and do all our work, but the seventh is a Sabbath to You, the Lord our God.*

- *Thank You Lord that we will honor our father and mother so that we may live long in the land.*

- *Thank You Lord that we will not murder.*

- *Thank You Lord that we shall not commit adultery.*

- *Thank You Lord that we will not steal.*

- *Thank You Lord that we will not give false testimony (lie) against our neighbor.*

- *Thank You Lord that we will not covet our neighbors' house, or his wife/husband or his man servant or his maid servant or anything that belongs to our neighbor.*

Exodus 20:17

In the name of Jesus Christ
(See Prayer of Repentance page 22)

FAITH AND STRENGTH

'Now faith is the assurance of things hoped for, the conviction of things not seen. For by it men of old gained approval.'

Hebrews 11:1

'... and without faith it is impossible to please Him, for he who comes to God must believe that He is, and that He is a rewarder of those who seek Him.'

Hebrews 11:6

Thank You Lord that they/we will trust You with all their/our heart, and they/we will not lean on their/our own understanding. In all their/our ways they/we will acknowledge You, and You will make their/our paths straight. In the name of Jesus Christ.

Proverbs 3:5-6

Thank You Lord that these people will not waver in unbelief, but grow strong in faith, giving glory to God. In the name of Jesus Christ.

Romans 4:20

Thank You Lord that their faith is greatly enlarged. In the name of Jesus Christ.

2 Thessalonians 1:3

Thank You Lord that their faith should not stand on the wisdom of man, but on the power of God. In the name of Jesus Christ.

1 Corinthians 2:5

Thank You Lord that You will give strength to them, and bless them with peace. In the name of the Jesus Christ.

Psalm 29:11

Thank You Lord that You have strengthened us, because You considered us faithful, putting us into service. In the name of Jesus Christ.

1 Timothy 1:12

Thank You Lord they will trust in You at all times, and pour out their heart before You, for You are a refuge for them. In the name of Jesus Christ.

Psalm 62:8

Thank You Lord that on the day they called You, You did answer them; You did make them bold with strength in their soul. In the name of Jesus Christ.

Psalm 138:3

Thank You Lord that You are faithful, and You will strengthen and protect them from the evil one. In the name of Jesus Christ.

2 Thessalonians 3:3

Thank You Lord that they walk by faith, not by sight. In the name of Jesus Christ.

2 Corinthians 5:7

Thank You Lord that they can finally be strong in You, and in the strength of Your might. In the name of Jesus Christ.

Ephesians 6:10

Thank You Lord that You will grant Your strength to Your servants. In the name of Jesus Christ.

Psalm 86:16

Thank You Lord for letting them draw near to You with a sincere heart in full assurance of faith, having their hearts sprinkled clean from an evil conscience and their bodies washed with pure water. In the name of Jesus Christ.

Hebrews 10:22

Thank You Lord that I can do all things through Christ who strengthens me. In the name of Jesus Christ.

Philippians 4:13

Thank You Lord that all of these people will seek first the kingdom of God, and Your righteousness and all will be added unto them. In the name of Jesus Christ.

Matthew 6:33

Thank You Lord that You have the power to do what You promised. In the name of Jesus Christ.

Romans 4:21

Blessed are You Lord, because You have heard the voice of our supplication. You are our strength and our shield; our hearts trust in You and we are helped. Therefore our hearts exult, and with our song we will thank You. You are our strength, and You are a saving defence to Your anointed. Save Your people, and bless Your inheritance, be our shepherd also, and carry us forever. In the name of Jesus Christ.

Psalm 28:6-9

Thank You Lord that strength and dignity are their clothing. In the name of Jesus Christ.

Proverbs 31:25

Thank You Lord that You have girded us with strength for battle; You have subdued under us those who rose up against us. In the name of Jesus Christ.

Psalm 18:39

Thank You Lord that You gird us with strength, and make our way blameless. In the name of Jesus Christ.

Psalm 18:32

Thank You Lord that You will give us faith and knowledge resting on the hope of eternal life which God who does not lie, promised before the beginning of time. In the name Jesus Christ.

Titus 2:12

Thank You Lord that You will give strength to the weary, and increase the power of the weak. Even youth grow tired and weary, and young men stumble and fall; but those who hope in the Lord will renew our/their strength. We/they will soar on wings of eagles; we/they will run and not grow weary; we/ they will walk and not faint. In the name Jesus Christ.

Isaiah 40:29-31

Thank You Lord that they/we will flourish like the palm tree, and grow like a cedar in Lebanon. We are planted in the house of the Lord. We flourish in the courts of our God. In old age we still produce fruit; we are always green and full of sap, showing that the Lord is upright; The Lord is our rock and there is no unrighteousness in Him. In the name of Jesus Christ.

Psalm 92:12-15

JOY AND PEACE

Thank You Lord that You will put gladness in their/our hearts. In the name of Jesus Christ.

Psalm 4:7

Thank You Lord that those who look to You, Lord, are radiant, and their faces are not ashamed. In the name of Jesus Christ.

Psalm 34:5

Thank You Lord that the God of hope fills all of us with all joy and peace in believing that we may abound in hope by the power of the Holy Spirit. In the name of Jesus Christ.

Romans 15:13

Thank You Lord that we who love Your law have great peace, and nothing causes us to stumble. In the name of Jesus Christ.

Psalm 119:165

Thank You Lord that the ransomed of the Lord will return, and come with joyful shouting to Zion, with everlasting joy upon our heads. We will find gladness and joy, and sorrow and sighing will flee away. In the name of Jesus Christ.

Isaiah 35:10

Thank You Lord that You will make known to us the path of life; in Your presence is fullness of joy; in Your right hand there are pleasures for evermore. In the name of Jesus Christ.

Psalm 16:11

Thank You Lord that the Lord our God is in our midst, a victorious warrior. You will exult over us with joy. In the name of Jesus Christ.
Zephaniah 3:17

Thank You Lord that we will listen to You, and we will live securely, and we will be at ease from the dread of evil. In the name of Jesus Christ.

Proverbs 2:33

Thank You Lord that You have established peace for us. In the name of Jesus Christ.

Isaiah 26:12

Thank You Lord that we will let the peace of Christ rule in our hearts. In the name of Jesus Christ.

Colossians 3:15

Thank You Lord that You will continually grant us peace in every circumstance. In the name of Jesus Christ.

2 Thessalonians 3:16

Thank You Lord that we can cast all our anxiety upon You, because You care for us. In the name of Jesus Christ.

1 Peter 5:7

Thank You Lord that in peace we will both lie down and sleep, for You alone will make us dwell in safety. In the name of Jesus Christ.

Psalm 4:8

Thank You Lord that Your presence will go with us and You will give us rest. In the name of Jesus Christ.

Exodus 33:14

(The above scriptures are wonderful for babies and small children)

Thank You Lord that our mouths are filled with laughter, and our tongues with joyful shouting; we will say among the nations, the Lord has done great things for us, the Lord has done great things. We are glad. In the name of Jesus Christ.

Psalm 126:2-3

Thank You Lord that peace and love with faith will be given to us from You, God the Father, and the Lord Jesus Christ. In the name of Jesus Christ.

Ephesians 6:23

Thank You Lord, we have loved righteousness and hated wickedness; therefore, You have anointed us with the oil of joy above all fellows. In the name of Jesus Christ.

Psalm 45:7

Thank You Lord that You have given us rest on every side, there is neither adversary nor misfortune. In the name of Jesus Christ.

1 Kings 5:4

Thank You Lord that You will satisfy us in the morning with Your loving kindness that we may sing for joy and be glad all our days. In the name of Jesus Christ.

Psalm 90:14

Thank You Lord that we will go out with joy, and be led forth with peace; the mountains will break forth into shouts of joy before us, and all the trees of the fields will clap their hands. In the name of Jesus Christ.

Isaiah 55:12

Thank You Lord that You will comfort Zion (us). You will comfort all our waste places. And our wilderness You will make like Eden, and our desert like the garden of the Lord. Joy and gladness will be found in us, thanksgiving and a sound of a melody. In the name of Jesus Christ.

Isaiah 51:3

Thank You Lord that when anxiety was great within us, Your consolation brought joy to our soul. In the name of Jesus Christ.

Psalm 94:19

Thank You Lord that our hearts are glad, and our glory rejoices; our flesh will dwell securely. In the name of Jesus Christ.

Psalm 16:9

Thank You Lord that You will fill our hearts with joy. In the name of Jesus Christ.

Acts 14:17

Thank You Lord that You have turned all our mourning into joy. You have loosed our sackcloth, and girded us with gladness, that our souls may sing praises to You and not be silent. Oh Lord we give thanks to You forever. In the name of Jesus Christ.

Psalm 30:11

Thank You Lord that our hearts rejoice in You, because we trust in Your holy name. In the name of Jesus Christ.

Psalm 33:21

Thank You Lord that the steadfast of mind You will keep in perfect peace, because we trust in You. In the name of Jesus Christ.

Isaiah 26:3

Thank You Lord that I am greatly encouraged; in all troubles my joy knows no bounds. In the name of Jesus Christ.

2 Corinthians 7:4

Thank You Lord that that You will bring joy to Your servant, for to You, O Lord, I lift up my soul. In the name of Jesus Christ.

Psalm 86:4

PROTECTION

Thank You Lord that in peace they/we will both lie down and sleep, for You alone make them/us to dwell in safety. In the name of Jesus Christ.

Psalm 4:8

Thank You Lord that You will protect them from all evil; You will keep their soul. In the name of Jesus Christ.

Psalm 121:7

Thank You Lord that You will guard their going out and their coming in from this time forth and forever. In the name of Jesus Christ.

Psalm 121:8

Thank You Lord that as the mountains surround Jerusalem, so will You surround Your people from this time forth and forever. In the name of Jesus Christ.

Psalm 125:2

Thank You Lord that You will give Your angels charge concerning them, to guard them in all their ways. They will bear them up in their hands, lest they strike their foot against a stone. In the name of Jesus Christ.

Psalm 91:11-12

Thank You Lord that no evil will befall them, nor any plague come near their tent. In the name of Jesus Christ.

Psalm 91:10

Thank You Lord that You will deliver them from the snare of the trapper, and from the deadly pestilence. You will cover them with Your pinions, and under Your wings they may seek refuge. Thank You that Your faithfulness is a shield and bulwark. In the name of Jesus Christ.

Psalm 91:3-4

Thank You Lord that You will put Your foot on all the necks of their enemies. In the name of Jesus Christ.

Joshua 10:25

Thank You Lord that these people will listen to You and live securely, and shall be at ease from the dread of evil. In the name of Jesus Christ.

Proverbs 1:33

Thank You Lord that You save the children of the needy, and crush the oppressor. In the name of Jesus Christ.

Psalm 72:4

Thank You Lord that it is You who blesses the righteous man, You surround him with favor as with a shield. In the name of Jesus Christ.

Psalm 5:12

Thank You that You, Holy Father, will protect them/us by the power of Your name, the name You gave Jesus, so they/ we may be one as You and Jesus are one. In the name of Jesus Christ.

John 17:11

Thank You Lord that the angel of Your presence will save us. In the name of Jesus Christ.

Isaiah 63:9

Thank You Lord that You are our hiding place; You preserve us from trouble; You surround us with songs of deliverance. In the name of Jesus Christ.

Psalm 32:7

Thank You Lord that You will protect us from the evil one. In the name of Jesus Christ.

John 17:15

Thank You Lord that they will not be ashamed in the time of evil; and in the days of famine they will have abundance. In the name of Jesus Christ.

Psalm 37:19

Thank You Lord that You help them and deliver them; You deliver them from the wicked and save them, because they take refuge in You. In the name of Jesus Christ.

Psalm 37:40

Thank You Lord that You hide us in the secret place from the conspiracy of man. You keep us secretly in a shelter from the strife of tongues. In the name of Jesus Christ.

Psalm 31:20

Thank You Lord that You will rise up Oh Lord, and our enemies will be scattered and our foes will flee before us. In the name of Jesus Christ.

Numbers 10:35

Thank You Lord that we will trust in You, Oh Lord. We will say, 'You are our God'. Our times are in Your hands. Deliver us from the hand of our enemies and from those who persecute us. In the name of Jesus Christ.

Psalm 31:14-15

Thank You Lord that the loving kindness of the Lord is from everlasting to everlasting on those who fear You, and Your righteousness to children's children, to those who keep Your covenant and who remember Your precepts to do them. In the name of Jesus Christ.

Psalm 103:17-18

Thank You Lord that You wondrously show Your loving kindness to our nation, Oh Savior of those who take refuge at Your right hand from those who rise up against us. In the name of Jesus Christ.

Psalm 17:7

Thank You Lord that You are a righteous God who searches minds and hearts, Thank You Lord that You will bring to an end the violence of the wicked and make the righteous secure. In the name Jesus Christ.

Psalm 7:9

Thank You Lord that should evil come upon us, the sword or judgement or pestilence or famine, we will stand before this house and You (for Your name is in this house) and we will cry to You, Oh Lord, in our distress, and You will hear and deliver us! In the name of Jesus Christ.

II Chronicles 20:9

All of Psalm 37!

Thank You Lord that Your eyes are on those who fear You, on those whose hope is in Your unfailing Love to deliver them/us from death and keep us alive in famine. In the name of Jesus Christ.

Psalm 33:18-19

COMFORT

Thank You Lord that this is their/our comfort in their/our affliction, that Your word has revived them/us. In the name of Jesus Christ.

Psalm 119:50

Thank You Lord that You, even You, are the one that comforts them. In the name of Jesus Christ.

Isaiah 51:12

Thank You Lord for comforting all who mourn. In the name of Jesus Christ.

Isaiah 61:2

Thank You Lord that You will turn their mourning into joy and will comfort them and make them rejoice from their sorrow. In the name of Jesus Christ.

Jeremiah 31:13

Thank You Lord that they will cry to You in their distress and You will hear and deliver them. In the name of Jesus Christ.

2 Chronicles 20:9

Thank You Lord that these people will trust in You at all times. They will pour out their hearts before You. Thank You Lord that You are a refuge for them. In the name of Jesus Christ.

Psalm 62:8

Thank You Lord that You will command Your loving kindness in the daytime, and Your song will be with them in the night. In the name of Jesus Christ.

Psalm 42:8

Thank You Lord that You are their refuge and strength, a very present help in trouble. Therefore, they will not fear, though the earth should change, and though the mountains slip into the heart of the sea. In the name of Jesus Christ.

Psalm 46:1-2

Thank You Lord that when they lie down, they will not be afraid; when they lie down, their sleep will be sweet. They will not be afraid of sudden fear, neither of the desolation of the wicked when it comes, for You will be their confidence and will keep their foot from being taken. In the name of Jesus Christ.

Proverbs 3:24-26

Thank You Lord that You will bring them out of their distress. In the name of Jesus Christ.

Psalm 25:17

Thank You Lord that these people will hope in You, for they will again praise You for the help of Your presence. In the name of Jesus Christ.

Psalm 42:5

Thank You Lord that You tell us that because You love us, You will protect us because we acknowledge Your name. In the name of Jesus Christ.

Psalm 91:14-15

Thank You Lord that You, even in our old age and gray hairs, You are God, You are the one that sustains us, You have made us and You will carry us; You will sustain us and You will rescue us. In the name of Jesus Christ.

Isaiah 46:4

SPECIAL NEEDS

All of these Scriptures can be prayed for people with all kinds of special needs. However, some of the Scriptures are particularly helpful for the needs noted in brackets.

Thank You Lord that we will find gladness and joy, and sorrow and sighing will flee away. In the name of Jesus Christ.

Isaiah 35:10

Thank You Lord that You have stored up goodness for those who fear You, which You have wrought for those who take refuge in You before the sons of men. You hide them in the secret place of Your presence from the conspiracy of man: You keep them secretly in a shelter from the strife of tongues. In the name of Jesus Christ. *(Court cases)*

Psalm 31:19-20

Thank You Lord that the enemy will not deceive them nor the son of wickedness afflict them — You will crush their adversaries before them, and strike those who hate them. In the name of Jesus Christ.

Psalm 89:22-23

Thank You Lord that these people's times are in Your hands. Deliver them from the hand of their enemy, and from those who persecute them. Make Your face shine upon them, save them in Your loving kindness. In the name of Jesus Christ. *(Court cases)*

Psalm 31:16-15

Thank You Lord for satisfying their years with good things, so that their youth is renewed like the eagles. In the name of Jesus Christ. *(For health)*

Psalm 103:5

Thank You Lord that You will be the stability of their times, a wealth of salvation, wisdom, and knowledge, and the fear of the Lord is their treasure. In the name of Jesus Christ.

Isaiah 33:6

Thank You Lord that they will not be put to shame, Oh Lord, for they call upon You. Let the wicked be put to shame. Let them be silent in Sheol. Let lying lips be dumb, which speak arrogantly against the righteous with pride and contempt. In the name of Jesus Christ. *(Court cases)*

Psalm 31:17-18

Thank You Lord that all of these have faith which is the assurance of things hoped for, the conviction of things not seen, and without faith it is impossible to please God, for he who comes to God must believe that He is, and that He is a rewarder of those who seek Him. In the name of Jesus Christ.

Hebrews 11:1, 6

Thank You Lord that You will make them and the places around Your hill a blessing. And You will cause showers to come down in their season: they will be showers of blessings. In the name of Jesus Christ.

Ezekiel 34:26

Thank You Lord that the mind of the hasty will discern truth, and the tongue of the stammerers will hasten to speak clearly. In the name of Jesus Christ. *(For improvement in school work)*

Isaiah 32:4

Thank You Lord that they will draw near with confidence to the throne of grace, that they may receive mercy and may find grace to help in time of need. In the name of Jesus Christ.

Hebrews 4:16

Thank You Lord that peace may be within their walls, and prosperity within their palaces. In the name of Jesus Christ. *(Financial blessings)*

Psalm 122:7

Thank You Lord that it is written that it is good that they prosper and be in health just as their souls prosper. In the name of Jesus Christ. *(Physical, spiritual, financial blessings)*

3 John 1:2

Thank You Lord that You will supply all of their needs according to Your riches in glory. In the name of Jesus Christ.

Philippians 4:19

Thank You Lord that they will seek first the kingdom of God, and Your righteousness and all things will be added unto them. In the name of Jesus Christ.

Matthew 6:33

Thank You Lord that You will teach them to profit and show them the way in which to go. In the name of Jesus Christ. *(For jobs)*

Isaiah 48:17

Thank You Lord that You will protect them from all evil; You will keep their soul. In the name of Jesus Christ.

Psalm 121:7

Thank You Lord that the Spirit of the Lord will rest upon them. The spirit of wisdom and understanding, the spirit of counsel and strength, the spirit of knowledge, and the fear of the Lord. In the name of Jesus Christ.

Isaiah 11:2

Thank You Lord that You will deal bountifully with them. In the name of Jesus Christ.

Psalm 13:6

Thank You Lord that You have granted to them everything pertaining to life and godliness through the true knowledge of Him who called them by His own glory and excellence. In the name of Jesus Christ.

2 Peter 1:3

Thank You Lord that their flesh will grow lean without fatness. In the name of Jesus Christ.

Psalm 109:24

Thank You Lord that You will accomplish what concerns them. In the name of Jesus Christ.

Psalm 138:8

Thank You Lord that the angel of the Lord encamps around those who fear You, and rescues them. In the name of Jesus Christ.

Psalm 34:26

Thank You Lord that You have brought them forth also into a broad place; You rescued them, because You delighted in them. In the name of Jesus Christ.

Psalm 18:19

Thank You Lord that You will lift them above those who rise up against them. In the name of Jesus Christ. *(Court cases, legal matters)*

Psalm 18:48

Thank You Lord of Hosts that You said; 'bring the whole tithe into the storehouse, so that there may be food in My house, and test Me now in this, if I will not open for you the windows of heaven, and pour out for you a blessing until it overflows. Then I will rebuke the devourer for you, so that it may not destroy the fruits of the ground; nor will your vine in the field cast its grapes,' says the Lord of Hosts. In the name of Jesus Christ.

Malachi 3:10

This is the greatest verse for people in financial difficulty. No matter how little a person has, the Lord wants the first 10%! It is not the money; He is begging for absolute faith in Him, and an opportunity to show us what He is capable of doing for us!

Thank You Lord that we will do everything You have said. We will obey! In the name of Jesus Christ.

Exodus 24:7

Thank You Lord that You will give rain in its season, both the autumn rain and the spring rain and You will keep us for the appointed weeks of the harvest. In the name of Jesus Christ. *(To keep our land balanced with rain and good crops)*

Jeremiah 5:24

Thank You Lord that You will cause Your people to be very fruitful, and make them stronger than their adversaries. In the name of Jesus Christ. *(Great for court cases)*

Psalm 105:24

Thank You Lord that the desire of the righteous will be granted. In the name of Jesus Christ. *(Jobs, homes, mates, children)*

Proverbs 10:24

Thank You Lord that You will make the barren woman abide in the house as a joyful mother of children. Praise the Lord. In the name of Jesus Christ. *(For those wanting to conceive a child)*

Psalm 113:9

Thank You Lord that You will give us rain for the seed which we will sow in the ground, and bread from the yield of the ground, and it will be rich and plenteous. In the name of Jesus Christ.

Isaiah 30:23

Thank You Lord that You will deal bountifully with Your servants, that they may live and keep Your Word. In the name of Jesus Christ. *(Financial blessing)*

Psalm 119:17

Thank You Lord that no weapon formed against them will prosper and every tongue that accuses them in judgment, You will condemn. This is the heritage of the servants of the Lord, and their vindication is from You, Lord. In the name of Jesus Christ. *(Court cases)*

Isaiah 54:17

Thank You Lord that there remains a Sabbath rest for the people of God. For we who have entered Your rest have ourselves also rested from our works, as You did from Yours. Let us therefore be diligent to enter that rest, lest anyone fall. In the name of Jesus Christ.

Hebrews 4:9-11

Thank You Lord that they will sing to You, they will praise You, for You have delivered the souls of the needy ones from the hands of evil doers. In the name of Jesus Christ.

Jeremiah 20:13

Thank You Lord that You will cause a deep sleep to fall upon them, and they will sleep. In the name of Jesus Christ. *(Sleep and rest)*

Genesis 2:21

Thank You Lord that You will give them utterance and wisdom which none of their opponents will be able to resist or refute. In the name of Jesus Christ.

Luke 21:15

Thank You Lord that the beloved of the Lord will rest secure in You, for You shield us all day long, and the one You love rests between Your shoulders. In the name of Jesus Christ. *(Sleep and rest)*
Deuteronomy 33:12 (NIV)

Thank You Lord that You have given them their heart's desire and have not withheld the request of their lips. In the name of Jesus Christ. *(Jobs, homes, desiring a mate, children)*

Psalm 21:2

Thank You Lord that You have saved them from their adversaries, and You have put to shame those who hate them. In the name of Jesus Christ.

Psalm 44:7

Thank You Lord that in peace we will both lie down and sleep, for You alone, Oh Lord, make us dwell in safety. In the name of Jesus Christ. *(Sleep and rest)*

Psalm 4:8

Thank You Lord that when we lie down, we will not be afraid; when we lie down, our sleep will be sweet. In the name of Jesus Christ. *(Sleep and rest)*

Proverbs 3:24

Thank You Lord that we who dwell in the shadow of the Most High will rest in the shadow of the Almighty. In the name of Jesus Christ. *(Sleep and rest)*

Psalm 91:1 (NIV)

Thank You Lord that You grant sleep to those You love. In the name of Jesus Christ. *(Sleep and rest)*

Psalm 127:2 (NIV)

Thank You Lord that their souls will abide in prosperity, and their descendants will inherit the earth. In the name of Jesus Christ.

Psalm 25:13

Thank You Lord that a sound sleep from the Lord will fall on them. In the name of Jesus Christ. *(Sleep and rest)*

1 Samuel 26:12

Thank You Lord that they will sing to You, for You have dealt bountifully with them. In the name of Jesus Christ.

Psalm 13:6

Thank You Lord that You will command Your loving kindness in the daytime, and Your song will be with us in the night. In the name of Jesus Christ. *(Sleep and rest)*

Psalm 42:8

Thank You Lord that You are their Judge, You are their Lawgiver, You are their King, and You will save them. In the name of Jesus Christ.

Isaiah 33:22

Thank You Lord that You cover the sky with clouds and You supply the earth with rain. In the name of Jesus Christ.

Isaiah 32:18

Thank You Lord that the sleep of the working man is pleasant. In the name of Jesus Christ. *(Sleep and rest)*

Ecclesiastes 5:12

Thank You Lord that You will fight for them, they need only be still. In the name of Jesus Christ.

Exodus 13:14

Thank You Lord that You know the plans that You have for us, plans for welfare and not for calamity, plans to give us hope and a future. Then we will call upon You and come and pray to You, and You will listen to us. And we will seek You and find You, when we search for You with all our heart. In the name of Jesus Christ.

'I will be found by you,' declares the Lord.

Jeremiah 29:11-14

Thank You, Lord, that thus far the Lord has helped us. In the name of Jesus Christ.

1 Samuel 7:12

Thank You Lord that You will equip us in every good thing to do Your will, working in us that which is pleasant in Your sight, through Jesus Christ, to Whom be the glory forever and ever. Amen In the name of Jesus Christ.

Hebrews 13:21

Thank You Lord that the lions grow weak and hungry, but those who seek the Lord lack no good thing. In the name of Jesus Christ.

Psalm 34:10

Thank You Lord that we will increase, we and our children. Thank you that we will be blessed by the Lord who made heaven and earth. In the name of Jesus Christ.

Psalm 115:14-15

Thank You Lord that in everything we do we will have great success, because the Lord is with us. In the name of Jesus Christ.

I Samuel 18:14

Thank You Lord that You have shown kindness by giving us rain from heaven and crops in their season. Thank You that You provide us with plenty of food and fill our hearts with joy. In the name of Jesus Christ.

GENERATIONAL HEALING

They shall be called oaks of righteousness,
The planting of the Lord, to display his glory.
They shall build up the ancient ruins,
The shall raise up the former devastation;
They shall repair the ruined cities,
The devastations of many generations.

Isaiah 61:3,4

Are there patterns of physical, emotional or spiritual illnesses in your family line; "the devastations of many generations"? Have you searched for healing of these problems only to have it elude you? Perhaps generational healing is the answer to your problems. God uses the ministry of generational healing powerfully to set people free from the sins, hurts and familial disease – "the devastations of many generations" – that sometimes come down to us through the past generations of our family lines. Those engaged in prayer ministry are used to having people come to them with hurts so deep that nothing they do seems to help. These difficult cases are like the people Jesus spoke of in the Parable of the Sower (Luke 8:4-15). The problems coming down through their family lines have caused the soil of their inner being to be so packed down that the word of God cannot take root in it. The hurts they have received have become like thorns and weeds that choke and strangle any attempts to grow emotionally or spiritually. The 'cares and riches and pleasures of life' overwhelm them and they cannot know peace, no matter how hard they try. This is a perfect description of those who can only be helped through the ministry we call 'generational healing.' Praying for the healing of those loved ones who have gone to be with the Lord is not anything new. We see a pattern of interceding for the deceased in both the Old Testament and the New Testament (Dan. 9:4-6, 20, Neh. 9:2,2 Mac 12:2-45, 1 Cor. 15:29, 2 Tim. 1:28, 1 Peter 3:18-19).

In healing of generations prayer we ask our Lord Jesus Christ to show us where the problems we see in our family line today began. As we do this, our Lord will often show us that the personal or family problem that is bothering us the most today had its beginning generations ago. Our ancestors may have sinned greatly themselves, or were terribly hurt when others sinned against them. Those great hurts and traumas have caused blocks in the family line that keep the healing power of Jesus from flowing into the family and bringing his peace. These blocks are only healed as a family member turns to God, asks forgiveness for the sins of the family and extends forgiveness to those who hurt them. We each need to also ask forgiveness for any way in which we, or other family members, have continued the sinful behavior. If we don't do this the problems will continue to aggravate people in the family line. So generational healing begins with our acknowledgment of a problem in our family and we are healed as we ask God to forgive all involved in that problem. *Forgiveness is the key to any healing*. If forgiveness is not forthcoming the pain and dysfunction will become much worse with each successive generation. If we have problems forgiving those who hurt our family members we ask Jesus to give us the forgiveness he has for them. When family members in the present generation turn to God with love and forgiveness in their heart and ask him to send the power of Jesus' shed blood into the hurting places in the family line, the painful effects of past sin and hurt are cut off. Then his healing and wholeness can be felt in the lives of present-day family members.

We each have a powerful enemy, Satan, who doesn't want our families to be healed and set free. So we need all of the prayer power we can get when doing generational healing. We never do generational prayers alone, we always ask one or two friends to pray with us. This gives us protection, discernment, and more prayer power. Before going into prayer we make sure we have all of the spiritual protection we will need. First we put on the full armor of God (p. 16) and pray the Deliverance Prayers (pp 25-26). The Scriptures for Intercessors are also very helpful (p. 14). Many of the present day problems we encounter have to do with people taking part in occult, satanic, Masonic, pagan or new age activities, so we also use the prayer renouncing occult activities (pp. 33-34). All prayers are from *The Sword of The Spirit*

After doing this, look over your family tree to see what problems need prayer. Focus on what you know, don't worry about what you don't know. If there are any places that you don't know about that need healing, Jesus will lead you to them. Jesus is our leader in every step of this ministry. He knows our hurts and those of past generations because all of history and every moment of time belong to him and he will send the Holy Spirit to bring into our minds everything that needs healing. We then become prayer warriors and lift up to him our entire family, living and dead, for his healing touch. As we do this we remind ourselves that we are seated with Jesus in the heavens (Ephesians 2:4-6). We are empowered by the Holy Spirit, praying before the throne of God (Rev. 13-14). As you can see from these verses our prayers are rising like incense before the throne of God day and night. God himself has called us to this ministry of intercession for our families. Because of this we know that if we continue to pray for them He will continue to heal them until they are completely whole.

If at all possible, it is very beneficial to have a service of Holy Communion (Eucharist, Lord's Supper, Mass) said for your family to break any bondage they might be in, or to take your family line in your heart and offer special prayers for them the next time you receive communion. In this way all of the power of Jesus' passion, death, and resurrection can be used to bring further healing to your family line.

The Prayer for Generational Healing is a prayer of forgiveness and healing for your family line. Before praying it, take the time to put yourself in Jesus' presence, standing with Him before the throne of God, with all of the company of heaven standing beside you and interceding for you and all in your family line. Now begin your prayer, confident in our Lord's love and power to bring you and all whom you love into complete healing. Always finish the prayers for your family by thanking God for the healing he is bringing to them, even when you don't yet see any. In this way you exercise your faith and open yourself and your family member up to further healing.

PRAYER FOR GENERATIONAL HEALING

• *Almighty and everlasting God, please gather together all of the generations of our family lines, past and present, that they may be healed of all hurts and freed from all bondage. We thank You for all of those in our family lines who passed down to us peace, love, and an ability to know You and Your Son Jesus Christ. Please send the light of Jesus into all of the sinful and hurting places in our family that people of the past and present generations may know the harm that they have done and come before You with repentant hearts.*

- *Those in past generations may have suffered pain and grief at the hands of others. Please send the blood of Jesus, shed for the forgiveness of sins, back into all pain-filled and grieving places, that both perpetrators and victims may be forgiven, healed and freed in Jesus' Holy Name.*

- *Those in past generations may have sinned against You and hurt others through physical, sexual, or emotional abuse. Please forgive them and break the hold these sins have on our family lines.*

- *Those in past generations may have sinned against You and hurt others by holding onto anger, unforgiveness and unrepentant bitterness. Please forgive them and break the hold these sins have on our family lines.*

- *Those in past generations may have sinned against You and hurt others by committing suicide, murder, or abortions. Please forgive them and break the hold these sins have on our family lines.*

- *We now commend into Your hands those in our family lines who committed suicide, were stillborn, aborted, or died untimely deaths, especially (insert names, if known). Receive them into the arms of Your mercy, into the blessed rest of everlasting peace, and into the glorious company of the saints in light.*

- *We now send our love and forgiveness back to those who hurt members of our family lines. We also send our love and forgiveness back to those members of our family lines who hurt others. We ask you to forgive them and bring them into wholeness and newness of life with You.*

- *We ask You to forgive those of us in the present generation and our progeny for any way in which we have given in to the tendency to sin in the same way our forebears did and we make the decision to forgive ourselves for this. Forgive us and restore us to life and health.*

- *We offer prayers for those present day family members who are in special need of Your healing touch: (insert names).*

- *In the Name of Jesus Christ and by the power of his cross and blood, we now break and make null and void any curses, contracts, covenants, hexes, spells, or pacts made against any one in our family lines, or by any member of our family lines against another person. WE break and make null and void any inner vows or bitter root judgments or expectations made against our family lines or by any member of our family lines against another person or family. WE place the cross and blood of Jesus, the symbols of his power and authority, between the past generations of our families and the present generation, thereby cutting off any evil that could in any way harm them, in Jesus Name. Amen.*

- *Almighty Father, we ask that you reveal to us any places in our family lines that need further prayers. Break the bondage of sin and ignorance. Look upon all of the people in our generational lines with compassion. Free them all, living and dead, that they might come before You in sure knowledge of Your love and forgiveness. Send into every dark and hurting place the love of Your Son Jesus Christ, that those in the past, present, and future generations may learn to live in wholeness of mind, body, and spirit, to the eternal glory of Your Holy Name, in and through Your Son, our Lord Jesus Christ. Amen.*

(From *Generation to Generation: A Manual for Healing*, Patricia A. Smith, 1996. Jehovah Rapha Press, Westport, MA, p. 48, 49,150) (This book can be ordered through patsmith04@ charter.net. Used by permission.)

SCRIPTURAL PRAYER
FOR GENERATIONAL HEALING

Thank You Lord You have rescued us from the domain of darkness, and transferred us into the Kingdom of His beloved Son, in whom we have redemption, the forgiveness of sin. In the name of Jesus Christ.

Colossians 1:13-14

Thank You Lord that You will rescue us from oppression and violence, for precious is our blood in Your sight. In the name of Jesus Christ.

Psalm 72:14

Thank You Lord that You will rescue us from our own people and You will open our eyes and turn us from darkness to light, and from the power of satan to God, so that we may receive forgiveness of sins, and a place among those who are sanctified by faith in You. In the name of Jesus Christ.

Acts 26:18

Thank You Lord that You again have compassion on us; You will tread our sins underfoot and hurl all our iniquities into the depth of the sea. In the name of Jesus Christ.

Micah 7:19

Thank You Lord that You help us and deliver us; thank You that You deliver us from the wicked and save us because we take refuge in You. In the name of Jesus Christ.

Psalm 37:40

Thank You Lord that You forgive all our sins and heal our diseases. In the name of Jesus Christ.

Psalm 103:4

Thank You Lord that You will save us from the hands of the wicked and redeem us from the grasp of the cruel. In the name of Jesus Christ.

Jeremiah 15:21

Thank You Lord that since the children share in flesh and blood, You too shared in our humanity so that by Your death You might destroy him who holds the power of death – that is the devil – and free us, who all of our lives were held in slavery by our fear of death. In the name of Jesus Christ.

Hebrews 2:14-15

Thank You Lord that we will not die for our father's sin. Thank You Lord that we have done what is just and right and have been careful to keep Your decrees, we will surely live. In the name of Jesus Christ.

Ezekiel 18:17-20

Thank You Lord that You tell us to repent! Turn away from all our offences; then sin will not be our downfall. Thank You Lord that we will rid ourselves of all offenses we have committed, and get a new heart and a new spirit. Thank You Lord that You take no pleasure in the death of anyone. We will repent and we will live. In the name of Jesus Christ.

Ezekiel 18:30:32

Thank You Lord that You will not remember the iniquities of our forefathers against us. In the name of Jesus Christ.

Psalm 79:8

Thank You Lord that I waited patiently for You. Thank You that You turned to me and heard my cry. You lifted me out of the slimy pit, out of the mud and mire; You set my feet on a rock and gave me a firm place to stand. Thank You Lord for putting a new song in my mouth, a hymn of praise to our God. Many will see and fear and trust in the Lord. In the name of Jesus Christ.

Psalm 40:1-3

Thank You Lord that we will not put out the Spirit's fire, we will not treat prophecies with contempt. We will test everything. We will hold onto the good. We will avoid every kind of evil. In the name of Jesus Christ.

1 Thessalonians 5:19-22

Thank You Lord that it is written that he who does what is sinful is of the devil, because the devil has been sinning from the beginning. It is written that the reason the Son of God appeared was to destroy the devil's work. Thank You Lord that the works of the devil are destroyed in each of these people that we lift to you this day. In the name of Jesus Christ.

1 John 3:8

Christian Healing Ministries (CHM) in Jacksonville, Florida, conducts Generational Healing Services several times a year. If you would like to know more about how you can participate in one of these services contact Christian Healing Ministries at www.christianhealingmin.org.

The classic piece of literature on the subject of generational healing, ***Healing the Family Tree,*** was written in 1982 by Dr. Kenneth McAll, a noted British psychiatrist and dedicated Christian (Anglican). Another very good book, much applauded by many in the healing ministry, is ***From Generation to Generation*** by Rev. Pat Smith. Rev. Smith's book (along with many other good resources on generational healing) is available in the bookstore of Christian Healing Ministries. Pages 160-164 of this book were written by Rev. Pat Smith. Francis MacNutt, Charles Kraft, and Derek Prince have all addressed the subject in their works and teachings.

BLESSINGS OF THE LORD

All believing Christians are entitled to these Blessings and Promises when they walk in the way of the Lord. Perhaps you will find these few scriptures refreshing and uplifting as we live in these stressful times.

It seems that most of God's blessings are cause and effect examples. 'You do that, and I will do this for you'. Always remember that one's choosing to believe and confess that Jesus Christ is the Son of God results in the absolute free gift of salvation. He does not expect or require that we 'do' anything to receive this free gift of eternal life. Salvation simply means saved, saved from death/hell, into eternal life with Jesus and God the Father. One can be the worst sinner on earth, continue to sin, and still believe in Jesus Christ as the Son of God and have salvation and the promise of eternal life.

However, when the sinner comes to Jesus, confesses his sin, repents, asks God's forgiveness, and forgives all the people and situations in his/her life with whom they have harbored unforgiveness, then God seems to open the pipeline of abundant life and blessings. When this happens a person truly becomes a 'new creation in Christ, the old things pass away and behold all is made new.' Remember, forgiveness and repentance are ongoing, lifelong processes – when these flow, the blessings flow.

It has been my observation that when people confess all of their sins before the Lord and forgive all who have ever caused them hurt or harm, and receive the Lord into their life as a 'heart' commitment rather than a 'head' commitment, then the power of the Lord flows through them and they experience that 'unrelenting love' that creates in them a deep desire to be obedient to God. Keeping His Word becomes a joyful way of life and is surely not a burdensome task. It is at this point that we begin to experience the Kingdom of Heaven 'eternal life' which is right here on earth.

SCRIPTURAL PRAYERS FOR BLESSINGS OF THE LORD

Thank You Lord that blessed are those whose lawless deeds have been forgiven and whose sins have been covered. Blessed is the man whose sin the Lord will not take into account. In the name of Jesus Christ.

Romans 4:7-8

Thank You Lord that You tell us that blessed are those who hear the Word of God and observe it. In the name of Jesus Christ. ... These are Jesus' own words!

Luke 11:28

The Word of God is the Old and New Testament. Believe me, there are no loopholes in the Bible! Jesus Himself tells us, 'Scripture cannot be broken' (John 10:35).

Thank You Lord that You tell us to 'pray for the peace of Jerusalem,' for those who do will prosper. In the name of Jesus Christ.

Psalm 122:6

Thank You Lord for redeeming Israel out of all their trouble. Thank You Lord that peace will be upon Israel. In the name of Jesus Christ.

Psalm 125:6

Thank You Lord that all who take refuge in You are blessed. In the name of Jesus Christ.

Psalm 2:12

Thank You Lord that You favor those who fear You, those who wait for Your loving kindness. In the name of Jesus Christ.

Psalm 147:11

Thank You Lord that the angel of the Lord surrounds us who fear You, and rescues us. Thank You Lord that we may taste and see that You are good. In the name of Jesus Christ.

Psalm 34:7-8

Thank You Lord that You will keep Your people from all evil. You will keep their soul. The Lord will guard their going out and their coming in from this time forth and forever. In the name of Jesus Christ.

Psalm 121:7-8

Thank You Lord that those who keep Your law have great peace, and nothing causes them to stumble. In the name of Jesus Christ.

Psalm 119:165

Thank You Lord that we can keep our ways pure by keeping them according to Your Word. In the name of Jesus Christ.

Psalm 119:9

How blessed is the man who takes refuge in You. Thank You Lord that Your Word tells us to fear the Lord, all of us Your saints; for to us who fear You, there is no want. The young lions do lack and suffer hunger, but we who seek the Lord shall not be in want of any good thing. In the name of Jesus Christ.

Psalm 34:8-10

Thank You Lord that Your eyes shall be upon the faithful of the land, that we may dwell with You, we that walk in a perfect way, we will serve You. In the name of Jesus Christ.

Psalm 101:6

Thank You Lord that in days of disaster we will not wither in days of famine, we will enjoy plenty. In the name of Jesus Christ.

Psalm 37:19

Thank You Lord that blessed are those whose way is blameless, who walk in the law of the Lord. How blessed are those who observe Your testimonies, who seek You with all their heart. They also do no unrighteousness; they walk in Your ways. You have ordained Your precepts, that they should keep them diligently. In the name of Jesus Christ.

Psalm 119:1-4

Psalm 91 is a beautiful outpouring of blessings and promises. Read it often for reassurance. God bless all of you every minute of the day and night.

Bless the Lord, Oh my soul, and forget none of His benefits; He forgives all our iniquities, He heals all of our diseases; He redeems our lives from destruction; He crowns us with loving kindness and tender mercies; He satisfies our mouths with good things, so that our youth is renewed like the eagle's. As far as the east is from the west, so far has He removed all of our transgressions from us. The mercy of the Lord is from everlasting to everlasting upon those that fear Him, and the righteousness unto children's children; to such as keep His covenant, and to those that remember His commandments to do them. In the name of Jesus Christ.

Psalm 103:1-5, 12, 17-18

Thank You Lord that in the day of trouble You will conceal Your people in Your tabernacle; in the secret place of Your tent You will hide us. You will lift us up on a rock. Our head will be lifted up above our enemies around us, and we will offer in Your tent sacrifices with shouts of joy; we will sing, yea, we will sing praises to the Lord. In the name of Jesus Christ.

Psalm 27:5-6

Thank You Lord that we shall serve the Lord our God, and You will bless our bread and our water; and You will remove sickness from our midst. There shall be no one miscarrying or barren in our Land, You will fulfill the number of our days. Thank You that You will send Your terror ahead of us, and throw into confusion all the people among whom we go, and You will make all our enemies turn their backs to us. In the name of Jesus Christ.

Exodus 23:25-27

Thank You Lord that You will bless us indeed, and enlarge our border, and that Your hand might be with us, and that You will keep us from harm, that it may not pain us. In the name of Jesus Christ.

1 Chronicles 4:10

ANSWERED PRAYERS

The following statements are samples of answered prayer from people who have called or written to Francis MacNutt's Christian Healing Ministries requesting prayer for their individual needs. When CHM receives a prayer request, our intercessors agree to pray for these requests for two months, praying in one accord the Scriptures in *The Sword of the Spirit*. We acknowledge the request of the individuals with a card letting them know we will be praying for them, and we request that they send in their praise report as they see the prayers being answered. We receive so many praise reports, and feel that God is answering so profoundly and so quickly because we are in one accord praying His Word. It really is exciting to watch!

It is my prayer that groups like ours will spring forth all over the world praying God's Word in one accord. If we pray He will heal! It is happening and I praise Him for it!

Inner Healing

'I lost my son in an auto accident in December and have been unable to pray since then. After receiving a copy of *The Sword of The Spirit,* I prayed the Deliverance Prayer and was instantly relieved of a deep depression. I now pray with ease and can praise the Lord once more.'

'I asked for prayer after being at the point of committing suicide, within days after requesting prayer, my life began to make a complete turn around. I cannot believe all the miracles that have taken place. Thank you so much for all the prayer.'

'I have been experiencing much freedom from depression since the beginning of March. I have been able to function at a better level at work. Did not notice PMS this month either. Only had a few low times. He is doing wonders. God bless all of you.'

'Your prayers turned my granddaughter's life around.'

'I had called and asked for prayers for a friend's daughter who had been given only days to live because of a very advanced case of anorexia. After I requested prayer, she began to get better, now she is greatly improved. Thank you so much for praying for her.'

'Thanks so much for the prayers on my behalf. They are having an effect. I have had numerous insights, healings, loss of fear, and more desire to be open and loving and an increasing desire for closeness. It is amazing to me that this short time should produce such results when I spent months working with a psychologist (in a church setting) with very little change. I am deeply grateful for your ministry.'

'I am now free of my addiction to prescription pills, bondage to satan, and an unforgiving attitude. Thank you so much for your prayers.'

'Gary has changed. Praise God! Thank you for your prayers.'

'My son was leading a homosexual lifestyle. I asked you to pray for him. I am so thrilled to tell you that he has changed, and is so much happier. He has given up his relationship, and finding himself interested in the opposite sex now. What a blessing. Thank you so much for praying for him.'

'I have not taken antidepressants for six months, I had taken them for 9 years. I am in a healing process for childhood sexual abuse. I am also being more productive at work. Thank you for your prayers.'

'Fran is making good progress in her battle over depression.'

'You prayed for me to face my anger and hatred toward the Lord, and I am so blessed that you did. He has raised me up into a greater joy, and He has given me a desire for more prayer. Bless you all and thank you.'

You prayed for my daughter who was heavy into alcohol, and suicidal. You name it, she was into it!! Her life is completely changed now. She is happy, alcohol free, and wants to serve the Lord. Thank you so much for praying for her.'

'My daughter is out of therapy, and off all her antidepressants after her mental breakdown. Thanks for the prayers.'

'I received inner healing for wounding from the Body of Christ. I received this healing during the Eucharist! Thank you for your prayers.'

'Your ministry has moved me. During the month you have been

praying on my behalf, I have completely forgotten about my compulsion. That is surely a major change – you just don't forget about 'compulsions', by the very definition of the word. I continue to be grateful, and am assured that my recovery will continue. Once again God has worked His healing in my life.'

'Thank you for praying for us. My children and I were incest victims. Jesus is doing a great job healing the three of us, physically, and spiritually. Joy has returned to this house. Thank you Jesus.'

'I have received much healing in regards to early childhood abuse, and my ex-husband's leaving. Thank you so much for your prayers.'

'Thank you for your prayers – the debilitating depression I have experienced most of my life has been eased somewhat. I am learning new ways to cope.'

'My thanks to you and all who prayed for me this past month. The most impressive thing I recognized, was that I had two very stressful experiences, and in neither case did the arthritis 'flare up'. I'm sure your prayers had fortified me, and I'm most appreciative.'

'I know I have written you before, and said thank you, dear one, but November a year ago, when you suggested that I write in my needs, little did I really know what God could do through Scriptural prayer. At the time, I was really in the pit, and had no faith, and no hope. First He set about restoring my relationship to Him, then He moved through my family, and finally He is working in my husband's life. Thank you all for praying for me.'

'Thanksgiving for inner healing. I feel like God has really done a work in my life.

'My daughter feels joy again after miscarriage, and has conceived a child that is healthy. Thank you for praying for her.'

'Praise! I asked for prayer for my friend last month. She has been without alcohol for twelve days now and has not mentioned suicide for two weeks. Emotionally, she is so much better.'

'God has been healing my sense of self. I am so grateful.'

'I requested prayer for a friend who had been in a living hell situation for years. He has now stopped drinking, and seems to be changing his lifestyle. The power of prayer seems to break through all barriers.'

'I am learning to praise God for all things, good and bad, and it is changing my life. I am listening to God and learning to obey. Thank you for praying for me.'

'I have been an intercessor now for about two months. In that time I've experienced some healing in the area of forgiveness, and I thank God for that sweet gift. Several relationships in my life that appeared terrible, have shown some signs of life. My mother's heart catheterization showed no blockages, which had her doctor really stumped, but we know she was healed through prayer. Thank you for the prayers.'

Special Needs

'I requested prayers for a safe pregnancy and delivery for my daughter-in-law whose pregnancy was questionable, even though the baby was premature, he is in excellent health. Thank you for your prayers.'

'We requested prayer for financial blessing. Shortly after that, we received a check in the mail for 2500 dollars, sender unknown. We couldn't believe it. How thankful we are. Thank you for praying for us.'

'Thank you for your prayer. Our house sold!'

'My self-employed son who is a painter, and makes minor house repairs went without any work for about four months earlier this year, your intercessors prayed for him, and he had so many work opportunities, he could not handle them all. Praise God, and thank you!'

'I called CHM with a prayer request for my son's job and marriage relationship. The next (very next) week, he went for an interview, and is now in his third week of work. He is even beginning a noon Bible study. God bless CHM for their prayers.'

'I wish to thank the Lord for financial blessings for our family. Also for a good trip north and good reunion with family and friends. I requested prayer for all of this, and He answered me.'

'Thank you for your prayers. I received contracts for 3 books from a Christian publisher and an invitation to write 4 more for next year from another Christian Publisher. Thank you for your prayers.'

'Thank you for your prayers. My son's wedding was beautiful, we have sold our house, and have a precious new grandchild.'

'My daughter got a job. Praise God!'

'In April, I asked you to put my son and husband on the prayer list for jobs. With joy I report that both got work last month. Praise the Lord. 'He does not always come in when we want Him to, but He always comes in on time.' Praise Him!'

'Thank you for prayers for my husband's job. He got the job he wanted.'

'Prayers were answered miraculously for two job situations in my family for which I am so grateful!'

'I would like to report a praise that I am able to work harder than I have for a year or more.'

'Praises! My friend's house sold! Thank you for praying.'

'Thank you so much for praying for me this past month. Since that time I have had two very promising things happen to me.'

'Thanks to God! Our daughter gave birth to a boy named Samuel because we 'asked the Lord for him' (I Samuel 1:20). Thank you all for your prayers!'

'God worked a mighty miracle in my daughter's job situation. Thank you for your prayers.'

'God has answered all of my prayer requests that I sent into you. Thank you.'

'My daughter got the new car she so desperately needed.'

'We have finally conceived a child. Thank you for praying for this.'

'Our house had been on the market for three years. I requested prayer for it to sell. I sent my request in the middle of January. The house sold February 10th. Thanks so much for the prayers.'

'We had asked prayer for our church to become 'more alive in the Spirit'. I cannot believe the change that has taken place. Our church is being renewed, simply through the beautiful music. It is a miracle to watch. Praise God, and thank you for praying for us.'

'We requested prayers for our business. The business has been overwhelming, in spite of the fact that this is supposed to be a very slow time of the year, and not to mention the recession. We really appreciate your prayers.'

'Praise! We had a bountiful year financially, and in many other ways too. Not many people can say that these days, right?'

'God has been faithful to me in fulfilling all my needs. I praise Him for your ministry. Thank you.'

Physical

'Our three year old son had the top of his fourth finger completely severed in a bicycle chain. I found the piece of finger, put it in ice and carried it and my son to the emergency room. The finger was sewn back on, but we were not encouraged by doctors about the results of the mending. After a few days the finger turned very black, and we were told he would lose the finger. My aunt, who is an intercessor for your group, called about this for prayer. Within days the finger began to come alive and grow perfectly normal. When the doctors removed the bandage they could not believe what they saw. Now the finger is perfect, with no trace of an injury. We thank you for your prayers.'

'My friend was diagnosed with pancreatic cancer. We immediately requested prayers. Two weeks after that he had two MRIs and there was no sign of cancer.'

'About three weeks ago I requested prayer for cluster migraine headaches; a new medication stopped my most recent one in its tracks. Hallelujah.'

'My mother has Alzheimer's, and every time I call you for prayer there is such an incredible change in her. Its so beautiful to watch. No anger spurts — no fits. Thank you so for the many prayers.'

(We also pray Deliverance and Inner Healing Scriptures for Alzheimer's patients).

'The many things I asked for have all been answered. Healing in a marriage. Five healed of cancer. Thank you for all the praying you've done for us.'

'Praise God for your prayers. We called about the baby who had a hole in his heart, was deaf, and doctors diagnosed as having AIDS. Now the baby is completely healed. I cannot tell you how thankful we are for all of your prayers.'

'I am a doctor and I was a doubting Thomas when I asked for prayers to heal a friend's inoperable brain tumor. She had been given 6 months to live. It is now four years later - the tumor has shrunk and she is doing great. Thank you for the prayers.'

'My oldest son has had a total remission of a spinal tumor. Praise God and thank you for prayer.'

'I appreciate your past prayers so much. I thank God for the healing that has begun. Thank you so much. I am so grateful after all these years of being so ill.'

'Kathy's surgery was fine. She had 23 years of cancer history, this time they got all of it. Thank you so much for praying for her.'

'Thank you for your prayers. I have had a wonderful healing, and physical renewal. The tumor was removed from my spine. I am able to walk and have feeling in my legs.'

'Daughter's test came out fine. I had asked you pray that the spot on her liver would be gone on a second check. P.T.L. it was! Thank you so much for praying.'

'Last summer our fourth child was born critically ill. Two brain surgeries followed and the problem could not be surgically corrected. My friend called CHM and asked that you pray for her. In Sept. we took her to a healing service. This was a first for us! The Pastor explained that the Bible declared that if we ask the Lord to heal her, and have the faith to believe that He would, He will. We experienced a tremendous peace and our faith grew. Thanking Jesus for His healing promises we prayed that He would manifest a sign of healing for us. Our baby got worse. We brought her back to the hospital. The doctor scheduled a third surgery, but told us that they did not think there was any hope. In the hospital room during admission procedures, we asked the Lord to take care of her. In a matter of minutes, the Lord healed her in my husband's arms. The doctors were shocked, saying there was no medical explanation. They insisted on keeping her for a 48 hour period. During this time she was looking around as though she was seeing everything for the first time. One month later the doctors confirmed that her bones had fused together, and the problem could not reoccur. Also when she was 10 days old the eye doctor told us that she was blind due to atrophy of the optic nerve. In October we took her to the eye doctor for a follow up and he confirmed that there was no longer any optic nerve atrophy, she could see. She has suffered no further health problems and is doing great. So many wonderful things have happened in our family during this time. We were all born again, and filled with the Holy Spirit. Thank You for praying throughout this time.'

'Last spring I asked for prayer for my adopted granddaughter, she had fetal alcohol syndrome. She has started to grow and learn. Thank you so much.'

'Thank you for your prayers. Cancer in remission currently.'

'My jaw was healed of TMJ at a healing service. Since changing therapists, the Lord is leading my recovery in a new way. Thanks for your prayers!

'My son's blood count has risen, and he has had no side effects from his medication. God bless you. Thank you for your prayers.'

'Praise God for your prayers in August. Total hip replacement has been completely successful.'

'My 89 year old sister had cancer surgery in June. She is completely healed. Praise God for His Blessings. Thanks to Him for CHM and your prayers.'

'Thank you for your prayers. My cancer is healed.'

'Miracle after miracle has been taking place as you have been praying for me while I am being healed of cancer. I am so grateful for all the prayers. I praise Jesus, my healer, and my redeemer. King of Kings and Lord of Lords is He.'

'My granddaughter's allergies have improved tremendously. She can breathe now for the first time. Thank you for praying for her.'

'I asked for prayers for a friend who was supposed 'to be dying' of cancer. I am happy to report that my friend is completely healed. God is so good. Thank you for your prayers.'

'I have been healed from my allergies, and work is going better.'

'My friend has recovered from a stroke. Thank you for praying for him.'

'My friend was 'healed completely' as she died peacefully tonight. She lived so much longer than doctors predicted.'

'My mother was in the hospital, very sick. Her doctor said there was no hope for her. She has now recovered, and is at home and doing very well. We are pleased, and thank God for His mercy and loving kindness.'

'My son is doing just great. Thank you so much for your prayers.'

'My friend has been free of leukemia for four months, and is rebuilding her blood and immune system. Please continue praying.'

'Thank you for your prayers. My recovery continues. I can now walk without a cane. Glory to God! May the Lord bless you in your ministry of healing.'

'My friend is home. Her recovery has been long, but on the onset, she was given only four to five days to live. The doctors admit surprise at her recovery. We feel that the prayer support really made the difference. Thank you for the prayers. We are so grateful.'

'I called in a request for my friend. He had a brain tumor, and the doctors told his wife he had only a few days to live. My friend is now praising God, and claiming a miracle because the tumor is much smaller, and the doctors are reducing his medication.'

'My bleeding ulcer is no longer bleeding. Thank you for praying for me.'

'A praise report for my two year old grandchild. Biopsy on kidneys was good. She was exposed to chicken pox, and did not get them. This could have been disastrous for her. Thank you for praying for her.'

'Thank you for your prayers. Our friend has been in remission of Multiple Sclerosis since August. Our deepest and most sincere thanks for your prayers.'

'I am now free of a pituitary tumor, addiction to prescription pills and mental illness.'

'I can't believe what happened after I asked for prayers. One miracle after the other. Thank you so much for praying for me.'

'Follow up on the last thanksgiving from last month. The woman we all prayed for in the church began very marked improvement within hours after we prayed. The Lord is really calling all people to pray for the people. I am convinced that if we are obedient and pray, He will heal.'

'I had all my tests done, and the tests showed no changes from the ones done six months ago. In other words, no new metastatic development, and no new disease. Thanks to God. God Bless each of you richly. Thank you for your prayers.'

'My friend was given only days to live, but after much prayer, is recovering beautifully. Thank you for your prayers. People are finding it hard to believe.'

'Last year I asked prayer for my husband who had a malignant tumor on his leg. He is doing great!'

'Several weeks ago I asked for prayer support for my son who had Crohne's disease. Now he is home for the summer, working at a gas station, and having as much fun as he can. He did very well at college and is on the Dean's list. Thank you for your prayers.'

'Thank you for your prayers concerning our adopting a child. As you remember we were very concerned when we found out about the mother's history and health. She had been on drugs, and had a very stressful pregnancy. I'm delighted to tell you Daniel was born in April and he is very healthy.'

'Thank you for praying for my friend. He is showing signs of improvement and has had a remission from cancer.'

'The rash is gone ... thank you for your prayers.'

'I thank you so much for your past prayers for my healing. I appreciate your prayers for me, and I am glad to say that, (thanks to your prayers), I am feeling better and better and (with you), I am thanking God for this healing.'

'My husband has had a miracle healing following your prayers. Thank you so much for praying for him.'

'It is with joy that I report that the prayers for my friend during the month of April have been tremendously helpful. She herself reported that she has received a miracle in the past two months – a sense of peace within, and the sure knowledge that whatever comes, she is in God's hands, and God's love will never leave her alone. The latest course of treatment and the prayers have resulted in her being cancer free for three months now. The most beautiful healing has been that of her despair and the depression. Thank you, thank you for your faithful, loving, healing prayers.'

'I thank God for the mighty way that Jesus uses our son, who has Downs Syndrome, to bring joy into the lives of others, especially his teachers.'

'My mother's lungs are healed.'

'Wonderful news! Both of the people, for whom I requested prayer, have had wonderful healings. The doctors are quite puzzled. Thank you for your prayers.'

'Thank you for praying for my daughter. She had a hole in her heart, now she is doing fine.'

'Thank you for praying for me. Please thank whoever prayed for me. It is a great joy to be able to do a normal day's work, and not suffer those exhausting episodes of irregular heart beats. Praise God!'

'I asked for prayers for my grandson for asthma. He is improving. The doctor did not put him on steroids, which they were considering. Praise the Lord!'

'I requested prayer for my friend with cancer. Kerry has improved in the last week. She has responded well to chemotherapy (no side effects). Thank you for praying.'

'Thank you for your prayers. Our praise is great. My husband is healed. He has felt better than he has in over 20 years. Thank you so very much for your prayers. What a miracle you have participated in.'

'I was diagnosed in early February with malignant mass on left breast. God is healing at a faster pace than the chemotherapy.'

'I am so grateful for your prayer group. I praise God for increasing health improvements after twenty years of chronic fibromyalgia.'

'You prayed for me for migraine headaches, that have plagued me sometimes as much as twice a month. I am almost totally free of them now. Thank you so much for praying for me.'

'My friend had her rods removed after a severe back injury. There is now a possibility that she will be able to walk. We appreciate your prayers so much.'

'My father was supposed to have heart problems, but after your prayers, the doctors could find nothing wrong with him.'

'My husband had a very questionable tumor that had to be removed. The doctors were sure the lump was cancerous. It was not! Thank you so much for your prayers for him.'

'Thanks for praying for my son. He has had no more seizures.'

'Thank you for interceding for my mother. She is much improved now.'

'My son had detached retinas, and at most the doctors said that with correction he would never see better than 20/85. Today he sees well with corrected vision of 20/25. I am so grateful for your ministry and the prayers that were prayed for us.'

'My daughter-in-law's unborn baby tested positive for Down's syndrome. I called you immediately for prayer. Two weeks later she was tested again, and everything came out negative. I cannot tell you how thankful we are. Thank you so much for praying for our needs.'

Salvation

'Last month I requested that you pray for salvation for my family members, including my bother-in-law, Larry. Well, Larry died in July. I thought he was not saved, and that all was lost. Many times I had prayed for him and witnessed to him about the Lord, but to no avail.

However, in my deep despair over the tragic thought of this, the Lord revealed in my spirit that Larry was saved, that somehow he reached out to the Lord on his own and that the Lord answered his prayer. Although I was not there to see it, I believed.

Almost immediately after receiving the revelation of Larry's salvation, I found in a pile of mail, your card saying that the CHM intercessors were praying for my request. I thank you and I thank God. I can't describe the joy that flooded my soul over the thought of him being in and with our Lord and Savior Jesus Christ.'

'God is so good. After twenty years of marriage, my husband has come to know the Lord, and joined our church last Sunday! Your ministry is greatly appreciated. You were there for me when I began my Christian walk. Thanks.'

'Thanks for your prayers, my father received the Lord at the age of seventy six!'

'I had asked for prayers for my daughter to come to the Lord. At one point she even cringed at the very name of Jesus. Today she not only praises the Lord, but prays, reads her Bible, and even prays for others. Thank you so much for praying for her.'

'Thank you for praying for my husband. He came to the Lord, and was delivered from many blockings.'

Deliverance

'I am a victim of severe childhood sexual abuse, and as a result have suffered most of my life with MPD, with very little result from counseling. I wrote you and asked for prayer, and you sent me a copy of *The Sword of The Spirit*. After a few weeks of praying the Deliverance Scriptures and Prayers, my personalities are beginning to merge, and I feel better than I have in years. Your prayers have meant life to me.'

'My son and wife have quit their job at a very evil establishment, and have started going to church. I thank God for your prayers.'

'I no longer have suicidal thoughts. It is wonderful to feel such peace. Thank you for all the praying.'

'My husband has agreed to treatment for anger and violent behavior. Praise God. Now we pray for a trained counselor and his healing in the process of therapy. I have prayed for this for twenty five years. Thank you for your prayers.'

'You prayed for me to face my anger and hatred toward the Lord, and I am so blessed that you did. He raised me up in greater joy, and He gave me a desire for more prayer. Bless you all and thank you.'

'Thank you for praying for my son. He had disappeared for two months, but now has returned, and is seeking counseling.'

'My friend is now off prescription drugs for depression, and has really had a spiritual renewal. Thank you for praying for her. Her life is so changed.'

'My friend has quit her occult activities altogether. Thank you for praying for her.'

'The Deliverance Prayer is the backbone of my prayer time. I'm so grateful to be an intercessor, and I praise Him that even with my total deafness, I'm not frustrated anymore. I just smile and read lips and get what I can out of a conversation.'

'The person for whom I asked you to pray has left the satanic coven, and is seeking counseling. We are so grateful for your prayers.'

Relationships

'My marriage is better than ever. Thank you so much.'

'After many prayers, my relationship with my son is coming around. Praise the Lord.'

'A relationship is beginning to heal between my son and me. Praise the Lord. Thank you for praying for us.' 'There has been a reconcil-iation in the families through prayer.'

'Thank you for your prayers. All were answered. Good report from doctors, healing in family relations, cure of stomach problems, and reconciliations. All seemed lost, but now has been restored!'

'The brokenness in our family relationships is being healed. It is just beautiful to watch. Thank you so much for praying for them.'

'After years of having a cloudy mind from many allergies, my mind is clear! My marriage (intimacy) is slowly healing. Praise God!'

'All divorce action has been stopped. I am so grateful.'

'I had asked for prayers for my brother and sister. They had not spoken to each other for ten years. They corresponded with each other the very month in which I had requested prayer.'

Wisdom – Guidance

'My praise report ... benefits of being an intercessor. God has blessed this effort, and I praise Him!'

'I asked prayer for wisdom for our daughter, she has begun to make incredible wise decisions on her own without being steered by either of us. It is so wonderful to watch.'

Peace – Joy

'My daughter feels joy again after miscarriage, and has conceived a child that is healthy. Thank you for praying for her.'

'After requesting prayer, I am experiencing a great inner peace. This is wonderful since for so many years, I have been in a state of absolute misery. Thank you so much for your prayers.'

'I have a three week old baby who was screaming nonstop. I found myself praying for him, but he was still fussy. When my husband prayed the Scriptures under 'peace' in your book, he settled down immediately.'

Nation

I recently read that "more Muslims received Christ as their Lord and Savior over the past ten years than any other time in history. A spiritual revolution is taking place in North Africa, The Middle East, and Central Asia. Even more astonishing is that many of these Muslims, including Shiites in Iran and Iraq are having personal encounters with the living Lord Jesus through dreams and visions. I call this a praise report because for years when we shipped out case loads of *SWORD OF THE SPIRIT*, we included prayer sheets that specifically asked the users of the book to pray for salvation and baptism of the Holy Spirit for all Muslims, Jews, Buddhists, and Hindus. This time frame of intercession for the Nations certainly parallels with the spiritual phenomenon which took place in the Muslim countries and in North Africa, and Central Asia. We have now included these people groups on the prayer request form on pages 11 and 12.

"We praise You Lord that You have promised that as we pray Your Word with all boldness, You will stretch out Your hand to heal, and signs and wonders will take place through the name of Your servant Jesus. In the name of Jesus Christ. We thank You Lord that You have kept Your promise to us."

In the last few years, we have prayed all darkness be brought into the light concerning the ethics of business institutions. I think the Lord has heard our prayer.

According to the *Washington Times*, the French are filling up the churches at an astonishing rate. France is usually considered a secular Nation. God is moving!

DELIVERANCE PRAYERS
from
The Sword of the Spirit
The Word of God

Praying God's Word for the Healing of Our Land

Joy Lamb

(Editions 1-6)

In the seventh edition of The Sword of the *Spirit the Word of God*, the original long Deliverance Prayer was deleted and replaced with a revised prayer.

However, we have had so many requests for this prayer in the past four years that we have decided to put it back in the tenth edition. This prayer is a culmination of various teachings on deliverance.

Deliverance simply means being set free from bondage-freedom!

When Paul was transformed by Jesus on the road to Damascus,

Jesus spoke directly to him and said, *"I am sending you to them to open their eyes and turn them from darkness to light and from the power of Satan to God, so they may receive forgiveness of sin and a place among those who are sanctified by faith in Me"* (Acts 26:17). I believe as prayer warriors we are to do the same, and these deliverance prayers, or "freedom" prayers, are invaluable tools with which to carry out God's assignment to us.

Praying these deliverance prayers seems to have brought freedom to so many. Please read the testimonies of the people who have used them beginning on page xi. We welcome your comments and praise reports. Please let us hear from you.

THE DELIVERANCE PRAYER

(Pray all 5 sections if time permits
...pray with authority)

In the name of the Lord Jesus Christ, and by the power of His blood and the Holy Spirit, I lift to the Lord myself, my family, my home, my neighborhood, my church, my work place, my city, state, nation, and the world, and each person for whom I am praying. I plead the blood of Jesus Christ over all of us for our protection. By the authority of the Word of God, it is written: "whatsoever is bound on earth, is bound in heaven; what is loosed on earth, is loosed in heaven."

Matthew 16:19

1. Binding Satanic Powers

Standing on the Word of God, and in the name of the Lord Jesus Christ, I bind all satanic powers, and all evil spirits, occult spirits, spirits of sin, spirits of trauma and familiar spirits, demonic forces, principalities, attributes, aspects, clusters, endowments, and satanic thrones. I bind all kings and princes of terrors. I bind all demonic assignments and functions of destruction, from any of the above demonic entities from outer space, the air, water, fire, the ground, the netherworld, and the evil forces of nature. I bind all interplay, interaction, communication and all their games between satanic and demonic spirits, out of and away from each and every individual's spirit, soul, mind, and body. In the name of Jesus Christ I declare all

189

of you demonic forces and spirits as weakened, defeated enemies of Jesus Christ. I sever all demonic spirits from any demonic ruler above these demonic spirits. In the Name of Jesus Christ, I revoke any orders given to any of these demonic spirits and demonic forces as it relates to the lives of all for whom I am praying. I bind all enemies of Jesus Christ present together, all demonic entities under the one and highest authority. I command that you all leave these people's lives, and go straight to the feet of Jesus Christ NOW!! Your assignments and influences in the lives of these people and areas are broken!! In the name of the Lord Jesus Christ.

I ask that God send the Holy Spirit, the holy angels of God, to surround, and protect each area and individual, and to seek out and cleanse with God's holy light all areas vacated by the forces of evil. I ask the Holy Spirit to permeate our spirits, minds, souls and bodies, creating a hunger and thirst for God's Holy Word, and to fill us to overflowing with the life and love of Jesus Christ, and His Holy Spirit. IN THE NAME OF JESUS CHRIST.

2. Breaking and Releasing from Curses

In the name of Jesus Christ, I rebuke all spells, hexes, curses, voodoo practices, witchcraft, occult, masonic and satanic rituals; occult, masonic and satanic blood covenants; occult, masonic and satanic blood sacrifices, demonic activity, evil wishes, coven rituals; all occult, Islamic, and coven fasting prayers (not of the Lord) and curse-like judgements that have been sent our way, and/or have been passed down through the generational bloodline. I command that they go back where they came from, and be replaced with a blessing. I ask forgiveness for, and renounce, all negative inner vows made by myself and by those for whom I am praying. I ask that Jesus Christ release us from these vows and from any bondage they may have held in us. In the name of Jesus Christ.

3. Freedom From Generational Sin

Thank You Lord that You will not remember the iniquities of our forefathers against us. In the Name of Jesus Christ. (Psalm 79:8)

In the name of the Lord Jesus Christ, and by the power of God's Holy Word, I take the sword of the Spirit and cut every person free from all generational inherited sins, weaknesses, character defects, personality traits, cellular disorders, genetic disorders, learned negative inner vows, and spiritual and psychological ties. I cut all bonds that are not of the Lord, AND PUT HIS CROSS BETWEEN us, our parents, our grandparents, our siblings, our offspring, our mates, (and any relationships that our mates have had with others in the past). I cut all bonds of the relationships of each one of us that are not of the Lord back to beginning of time, and by the sword of the Spirit, and in the name of Jesus Christ, I say that we are cut free, and we are free indeed. We are now free to become the children of God the Lord intended us to be. In the name of Jesus Christ.

4. Freedom from all evil of Mind, Body and Spirit

Thank You Lord that You will cleanse us/them of all defilement of the flesh and spirit that we may perfect holiness in the fear of the Lord. In the Name of Jesus Christ. (II Corinthians 7:1)

In the name of the Lord Jesus Christ, and by the power of God's Word, and the shed blood of Jesus Christ and the Holy Spirit, I bind the evil spirits of pride, judgment, rebellion, defiance, unforgiveness, envy, impatience, resentment, vanity, coveting, selfishness, idolatry, haughtiness, mockery, disobedience, arrogance, hypocrisy, denial, disbelief, guilt, shame, confusion, doubt, self-hatred, poor self image, rejection, persecution, prejudice. Possessiveness, anger, hatred, fear, timidity, passivity, control, unbelief, jealousy, division, disunity, distrust, deception, dishonesty, destruction, accusation, hostility, violence, dissension, torment, retaliation, vengeance, hyperactivity, competitiveness, envy, procrastination, stubbornness, strife, criticism, manipulation, materialism, shared secrets and shared confidences, betrayal, gossip, greed, jealousy, poverty and lack, revenge, adultery, divorce, separation, division, hypochondria, pain, infirmity of brain, eye, ear, nose, nerve, muscle, heart, lung, stomach, intestines, liver, bone, cell or blood, body chemistry, hormonal disorders or dysfunction, all diseases, cancer, AIDS, Alzheimer's, ALS-Parkinson's disease, Lyme's disease, and all infectious diseases, MS, fatigue, anorexia, bulimia, depression, oppression, suicide, schizophrenia, worry, anxiety, sleeplessness, ADD, nervousness, withdrawal, loneliness, isolation, ostracism, any negative spirits and all addictive spirits of gluttony, perfectionism, alcoholism, workoholism, busyness, nicotine, spending, shopping, gambling, frenzy, drug abuse, self abuse, exercise, sexual addictions, and sexual perversions, seduction, pornography, masturbation, lust, fornication, incest, lesbianism, homophobia, pedophilia, homosexuality, bisexuality, sexual inadequacies, frigidity, impotency, fear of sex, hatred of men, hatred of women, sexual impurities, immorality, abortion, promiscuity, materialism, witchcraft, familiar spirits, murder, games, deaf, dumb, blind, mute, and sleeping spirits, new age spirits, cult spirits, seducing and enticing spirits, and any occult spirits of darkness and death in all of us/them. I say that in the name of Jesus Christ, all these spirits are bound and I command that they go to the feet of Jesus Christ now! In the name of Jesus Christ.

Lord Jesus, I ask that You release the fullness of Your Holy Spirit to flood the places vacated by the darkness in all these people's minds, bodies, and souls. Please fill them with Your perfect love, joy, peace, truth, power, charity, humility, forgiveness, faithfulness, goodness, kindness, wholeness, wellness, health, trust, self control, good self-image, discipline, obedience, sound mind, prosperity, order, relinquishment, acceptance of themselves and others. Free them from all fear, guilt, shame, and all addictions, and fill them to overflowing with the light and life of Your Being. In the name of Jesus Christ.

5. Closing of Deliverance Prayer

Thank You Lord that You will awaken our sleeping spirits, and bring us into the light. Thank You Lord that You will transform us by the renewing of our minds daily in Christ Jesus. Thank You Lord that You will pour out Your Spirit on us, and reveal Your Word to us. Thank You Lord that You will give Your angels charge over us in all our ways. Thank You Lord that we believe in You, and from our innermost beings shall flow rivers of living waters. Thank You Lord that You will direct our hearts into the love of God and the steadfastness of Jesus Christ. In the name of Jesus Christ.

SHORT DELIVERANCE PRAYER

In the name of Jesus Christ, we lift to the Lord ourselves, our families, our homes, our neighborhood, our workplaces, our church, our city, our state, our Nation, and the World, and each person and area for which we are praying. By the power of Jesus Christ, and His shed blood, and the Holy Word of God, we bind the powers of Satan, the spirits, powers, and forces of darkness, the netherworld, and the satanic forces of nature. We bind any demonic assignments sent against any of the people and areas we just lifted to the Lord. We bind all interaction, interplay or communication and games between spirits as it may affect any of the people and areas in our spirits, souls, minds, and bodies, and command in the name of Jesus Christ that all these satanic and demonic forces go to the feet of Jesus Christ. Thank You, Lord, for sending the Holy Spirit of God and the holy angels to come and cleanse every place where Satan has had a foothold in the lives and situations of any of these people and areas, and to fill each cleansed area with the life and love of Our Lord Jesus Christ. In the name of Jesus Christ.

In the name of Jesus Christ, we rebuke and break any curses, hexes, spells, demonic activity, voodoo practices, coven fasting prayers, occult, masonic and satanic rituals, and all occult, masonic and satanic blood covenants and occult, masonic and satanic blood sacrifices, evil wishes, and any witchcraft that have been sent against us or passed down through the generational bloodline to us or to any of the people or areas for whom we are praying. We decommission any spirits sent against us and send them directly to Jesus Christ. In the name of Jesus Christ.

In the name of Jesus Christ, we renounce and ask forgiveness for any negative inner vows made by us or by any of the people for whom we are praying. We ask that Jesus Christ release us from these negative inner vows and from any bondage that these negative inner vows have caused us to experience within our spiritual and physical beings. We take the Sword of the Spirit and cut ourselves free from all generational sins, weaknesses, character defects, cellular and genetic disorders, and personality quirks or disorders back through one thousand generations. In the name of Jesus Christ. We cut all bonds of all relationships that are not of the Lord, and put His Cross between us and all relationships. We are cut free and we are free indeed. We are now free to become the children of God the Lord intended us to be, filled to overflowing with the power of the Holy Spirit of God, and the life and love of Jesus Christ.

We claim the shed blood of Jesus Christ, the son of the living God, over all that we have lifted to You for our and their protection. In the name of Jesus Christ.

The Lord rebuke you Satan! The Lord who chose Jerusalem rebuke you in all of the lives and situations we just lifted to the Lord. In the name of Jesus Christ.

Zechariah 3:1

For a more in-depth understanding of deliverance and how to deal with the evil that seems to have a grip on today's world, I would like to recommend *Deliverance From Evil Spirits: A Practical Manual* by Dr. Francis MacNutt. This book can be obtained from Christian Healing Ministries, Inc. Call 904-765-3332, ext. 219, or visit their website: www.christianhealingmin.org. The cost of the book is $18.99 plus tax and shipping. The book is also available in Christian Bookstores.

Text taken from *The Sword of Spirit The Word of God*
by Joy Lamb 6th Edition, Lamb's Books 3368 Lakeshore Blvd.
Jacksonville, FL 32210.

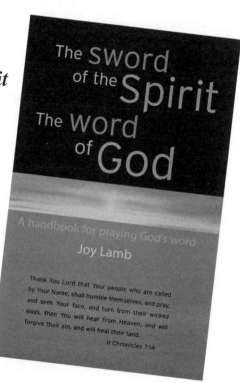

Lamb's Books • P.O. Box 380035 • Jacksonville, Florida 32205

To order using **PAYPAL** visit our website:
www.theswordofthespiritbook.com

To order using a **credit card** email for details: **lambsbooks2@gmail.com**

To order using **check or money order** - Please fill in the form
below and **MAIL FORM** together with your check or money order to:
Lamb's Books, P.O. Box 380035 • Jacksonville, FL 32205

ORDER FORM
PLEASE PRINT CLEARLY

Name _____

Address _____ Apt._____

City _____ State _____ Zip _____

Email Address _____

Phone No. _____

No of cases_____ **x $247.00** ($225.00 plus $22.00 S/H per case) = TOTAL _____
30 books per case ($7.50 per book)

No of ¹/₂ cases_____ **x $136.00** ($120.00 plus $16.00 S/H per case) = TOTAL _____
15 books per ¹/₂ case ($8.00 per book)

Please circle translation ENGLISH SPANISH

DATE OF ORDER _____ TOTAL REMITTED _____

** NO P.O. BOX NUMBERS – UPS ADDRESSES ONLY**
SHIPPING TO CANADA $50.00 • SHIPPING TO OTHER FOREIGN NATIONS $120.00
COPY OF RESALE TAX ID # REQUIRED IF BOOKS ARE TO BE RESOLD

The Sword of the Spirit the Word of God is **also available at Amazon.com**
in print and Kindle editions
lambsbooks2@gmail.com • www.theswordofthespiritbook.com

Thank You And May God Bless You
With Many Miracles

Thank You And May God Bless You
With Many Miracles

Formulario de Pedido

PARA ORDENAR COPIAS INDIVIDUALES DEL LIBRO EN ESPAÑOL:

La Espada del Espíritu, La Palabra de Dios
$15.00 por copia

Para órdenes escriba:

Christian Healing Ministries
438 W.67th Street
Jacksonville, FL 32208
1-904-765-3332 ext. 219

Correo electrónico:

www.christianhealingmin.org

Envíe su cheque personal o giro postal a nombre de Velez& Maymi, LLC
Manejo y Franqueo a E.U.A. -$5.00 por copia

Cantidad _____ X $ _____ = Total $ _____

Nombre _____ Dirección _____ Apt_____

Ciudad _____ Estado _____ Zip _____

Teléfono Núm. _____ Fecha de Orden _____

ORDENES AL POR MAYOR - Mínimo 15 copias
Lamb's Books, Inc.

3368 Lakeshore Blvd. • Jacksonville Fl 32210
electrónico: www.theswordofthespiritbook.com

Los precios al por mayor son ofrecidos a iglesias, grupos de oración, centros de consejería, librerías, etc. Una identificación de **impuesto de reventa (U.S.A. tax I.D.)** debe acompañar todas las órdenes al por mayor (Los grupos de oración pueden obtenerlo de su iglesia).

ORDENES POR CAJA (30 Libros Por Caja)

E.U.A. $225.00 + $22.00 manejo y franqueo por caja
Canada $225.00 + $50.00 manejo y franqueo por caja
Cajas de 15-29 libros - $8.00 por libro + $14.00 manejo y franqueo

Para órdenes internacionales, nos puede escribir a nuestro correo electrónicoo enviarnos un facsímil.

Núm. de cajas ____ x $225.00 + $22.00 M/F por caja = TOTAL $ _____ E.U.A.

Núm. de libros ____ x $8.00 (15-29) + $14.00 M/F = TOTAL $ _____ E.U.A.

Nombre _____ Dirección _____ Apt ____

Ciudad _____ Estado ____ Zip _____ Phone (____)_____

Tax I.D. para reventa # _____ Fecha de Orden_____

TOTAL REMITIDO $ _____

Gracias y que el Señor les bendiga con muchos milagros.

Personal Notes

Personal Notes

Personal Notes

Personal Notes